Praise for *I Shouldn't*

"*I Shouldn't Feel This Way* is a guidebook to finding peace and confidence in life. Dr. Alison's method guides readers on a path of self-awareness, compassion, and healing. Everyone needs this transformational book!"

— ALLI WORTHINGTON, BUSINESS COACH AND AUTHOR
OF *REMAINING YOU WHILE RAISING THEM*

"This book is like WebMD for your emotions. Dr. Alison's three-step method will help you diagnose your biggest feelings and their origins before they blow up your day. A must-read for all of us trying to make sense of our behavior and find healthier ways forward."

— LISA-JO BAKER, BESTSELLING AUTHOR OF *NEVER UNFRIENDED*
AND COHOST OF THE *OUT OF THE ORDINARY* PODCAST

"Learning to understand and navigate the complexity of your own thoughts and emotions is a lifelong journey. *I Shouldn't Feel This Way* is more than a map; it's your GPS. It will give you a thirty-thousand-foot view of the terrain of human emotion and show you which direction to go. Dr. Alison equips you with a straightforward framework to grow in awareness of your own thoughts and feelings, process them, and become a healthier you."

— CURTIS CHANG, AUTHOR OF *THE ANXIETY OPPORTUNITY*
AND HOST OF *GOOD FAITH* PODCAST

"Dr. Alison Cook possesses the extraordinary talent of distilling highly complex concepts around faith, psychology, and being human into practical and compassionate takeaways. With signature wisdom and expertise, *I Shouldn't Feel this Way* offers readers a nuanced and helpful view into what it means for us to honor the paradoxes and fullness of our God-given humanity. This is such a needed book, and it's an honor to recommend this important work."

— AUNDI KOLBER, MA, LPC, THERAPIST AND AUTHOR OF *TRY SOFTER*™,
TRY SOFTER™ GUIDED JOURNEY, AND *STRONG LIKE WATER*

"*I Shouldn't Feel This Way* compassionately helps us name our feelings, shed shame, and move through emotions—all while leading us into the loving embrace of the one who made us. Dr. Cook's wisdom-soaked words are not just accessible but also highly applicable to our messy, complicated realities. I highlighted my way through this illuminating book, and I'm grateful for how it speaks into my life as a parent, wife, neighbor, and friend."

— KAYLA CRAIG, CREATOR OF LITURGIES FOR PARENTS AND
AUTHOR OF *EVERY SEASON SACRED* AND *TO LIGHT THEIR WAY*

"Dr. Alison's latest book is perhaps her most down-to-earth and simple yet profoundly wise. Amid sometimes-complex therapeutic takes and terms and within the conflicts of our own lives, we need clear ways of naming what's happening, framing our reality, and braving our way forward. This is everyday wisdom born out of a holy imagination and offered with clarity and conviction."

— DR. CHUCK DEGROAT, PROFESSOR OF PASTORAL CARE AND
CHRISTIAN SPIRITUALITY, EXECUTIVE DIRECTOR OF THE CLINICAL
MENTAL HEALTH COUNSELING PROGRAM AT WESTERN THEOLOGICAL
SEMINARY, AND AUTHOR OF *WHEN NARCISSISM COMES TO CHURCH*

"Dr. Alison Cook gently and poetically equips readers with her simple but powerful framework to untangle the messy and conflicting thoughts that weigh so many of us down. She offers a refreshing approach to understanding guilt and a clear path out so that we can be free to live our lives with lightness, joy, and peace."

— DR. MORGAN CUTLIP, AUTHOR OF *LOVE YOUR
KIDS WITHOUT LOSING YOURSELF*

"True to Dr. Alison's anointed approach, in *I Shouldn't Feel This Way* she invites, disarms, equips, and renews the reader with a healthier and more loving understanding and acceptance of self. This book is imaginative in explaining and embracing our emotions and thoughts as part of the marvelous creation we are."

— MONIQUE GADSON, PHD, LPC, ASSISTANT PROFESSOR OF COUNSELING
PSYCHOLOGY AT THE SEATTLE SCHOOL OF THEOLOGY AND PSYCHOLOGY

"Dr. Alison has done it again with *I Shouldn't Feel This Way*! With the voice of a trustworthy guide, a wise teacher, and a close companion, Alison brilliantly shows us that feelings are not problems to be solved but gifts to be stewarded. And when stewarded well, our feelings can actually be an avenue of freedom, deep connection with others, and courageous action. *I Shouldn't Feel This Way* is a practical and profound treasure I will personally return to again and again and a resource I am eager to recommend to friends and clients in my counseling practice. Join me in filling the margins with notes. This book is a gift—a gift we all need."

— NICOLE ZASOWSKI, MARRIAGE AND FAMILY THERAPIST
AND AUTHOR OF *WHAT IF IT'S WONDERFUL?*

"When I feel lost in the forest of life's emotional upheavals and confusion, I'd settle to have a map that would help me gather my bearings and point me in the direction of home. But even more so, I would love to have a guide that is not only familiar with the map but knows the forest without even needing it—and will walk with me to keep me from getting lost again. With *I Shouldn't Feel This Way* we have our map, and in Alison Cook we have our guide. For those whose hearts are looking for the way home while making sense of the journey along the way, I can think of no better place to start."

— CURT THOMPSON, MD, PSYCHIATRIST AND AUTHOR OF
THE SOUL OF DESIRE AND *THE DEEPEST PLACE*

I
SHOULDN'T
FEEL
THIS WAY

I SHOULDN'T FEEL THIS WAY

Name What's Hard, Tame Your Guilt, and Transform Self-Sabotage into Brave Action

Dr. Alison Cook

NELSON
BOOKS

An Imprint of Thomas Nelson

Published in Nashville, Tennessee, by Nelson Books, an imprint of Thomas Nelson. Nelson Books and Thomas Nelson are registered trademarks of HarperCollins Christian Publishing, Inc.

The author is represented by Alive Literary Agency, www.aliveliterary.com.

Thomas Nelson titles may be purchased in bulk for educational, business, fundraising, or sales promotional use. For information, please email SpecialMarkets@ThomasNelson.com.

Each character or client in this book is based on a composite of multiple real-life stories and does not represent any one individual. Additionally, names, places, events, and details have been changed to protect confidentiality.

The information in this book is intended to be a source of information only. The author and the publisher assume no responsibility for any injuries suffered or damages or losses incurred during or as a result of the use or application of the information contained herein. Readers are urged to consult with their own physician or mental health professionals to address any specific issues.

Library of Congress Cataloging-in-Publication Data

Names: Cook, Alison K., author
Title: I shouldn't feel this way : name what's hard, tame your guilt, and transform self-sabotage into brave action / Dr. Alison Cook.
Description: Nashville, Tennessee : Nelson Books, [2024] | Summary: "Dr. Alison Cook uncovers the conflicting thoughts and emotions that keep us stuck and teaches us how to name, tame, and transform them into clear solutions that help us move forward in confidence"-- Provided by publisher.
Identifiers: LCCN 2023052914 (print) | LCCN 2023052915 (ebook) | ISBN 9781400234806 (trade paperback) | ISBN 9781400234813 (epub)
Subjects: LCSH: Guilt--Religious aspects--Christianity. | Psychology, Religious. | Confidence.
Classification: LCC BT722 .C83 2024 (print) | LCC BT722 (ebook) | DDC 248.4--dc23/eng/20240125
LC record available at https://lccn.loc.gov/2023052914
LC ebook record available at https://lccn.loc.gov/2023052915

Printed in the United States of America

24 25 26 27 28 LBC 5 4 3 2 1

To Joe,
the best Namer I've ever known

Contents

PART ONE

The Path to Clarity

ONE

The Crossroads

You're conflicted. Trapped between guilt and frustration.

Maybe your parents weren't there for you. Now they're aging, and you're all they have. You want to take care of them, but you're also angry about the care you didn't get.

Maybe your friend is constantly dumping all her problems on you. You feel like you should be a good listener. You want to support her. But you also dread seeing her name pop up on your phone.

Maybe it's your romantic relationship that hasn't been working for some time. It's not hostile, but you're barely speaking. You have a history together. You might even have kids together. You love this person. But you also hate yourself for the fact that you don't really like them very much.

You drift off into your imagination, dreaming of a different life. A different family, a different friendship, a different relationship. In your mind's eye, it's beautiful—everything you've dreamed of. You're valued, fulfilled, at peace.

Then the phone buzzes as a text jolts you from your reverie. "Hey, can you give me a call? I need your help!"

Instantly, you're pulled back into reality. You sigh, or swear, inside your mind. Defeat washes over you. And then comes the guilt.

What's wrong with me? you wonder. *How could I feel this way about my parent, my friend, my partner, my life?*

Just get it together, you chastise yourself. *Be grateful for what you have.*

You force yourself to flip the dream switch off and head back down the well-worn path that is your life.

Maybe it's not so bad. I really shouldn't feel this way.

But you do. Something happened inside that moment in your mind, the intersection of your fantasy and the life you actually have. It's hazy, a bit disorienting. But that place evokes a longing inside you.

What if you could feel that other way instead?

Valued instead of taken advantage of.

Fulfilled instead of frustrated.

At peace instead of conflicted.

Unbeknownst to you, that moment is an invitation—not to beat yourself up but, instead, to get curious. To ask yourself valuable questions as you seek understanding.

What's happening here?

What am I missing?

What do I need to understand about this situation?

The first step to confronting the challenges you face is to stop trying to tell yourself you shouldn't feel this way.

Pseudo Solutions

When we're stuck, our minds become a confusing tangle of mixed-up feelings and conflicting thoughts. This jumbled-up knot is a cry for gentle care and patient attention, but most of us haven't been given the tools required to unravel it. It's hard to navigate the challenges we face when the noisy clamor of *You should!* or *You shouldn't!* reverberates in our minds. We yearn for clarity, confidence, and conviction. Yet we're tangled up in our own inner conflicts, our own hurts, our own anger, and our own guilt messages. It's hard to sift through the complicated mix of doubts, fears, and real questions long enough and honestly enough to discover threads of real wisdom.

> THIS JUMBLED-UP KNOT IS A CRY FOR GENTLE CARE AND PATIENT ATTENTION, BUT MOST OF US HAVEN'T BEEN GIVEN THE TOOLS REQUIRED TO UNRAVEL IT.

We silently battle ourselves. And we silently battle against other people. We don't always know who we can trust. We want the truth. But we also don't want to be misunderstood. We feel hurt or confused by other people's behaviors, but we feel bound by our own loyalty, kindness, or misguided empathy. We want to be good to others, but sometimes being good to them tightens up the knots inside us.

And the noise all around us does not help us navigate complexity. Our social media feeds scream at us with ill-fitting positivity and guilt-tripping memes: *Choose happiness! Think positive! Be a giver, not a taker!* Faith communities offer spiritual solutions with equally ill-fitting platitudes: *Just have faith! Choose joy! Let go and let God!* Families and friends encourage us with well-intended half-truths: *Everything will be fine! You're doing great! Don't overthink it!*

We try to absorb these pseudo solutions and half-baked half-truths. And yet we continue to feel restless, uncertain, frustrated, and confused. *What if everything's not fine? What if we're not doing great? What if there's a reason we're overthinking?* We stay stuck in a swirl of a million truth-splinters that don't quite add up. They keep us fragmented from our bodies, our wisdom, and from real needs begging for our attention.

Quick-fix pseudo solutions are no match for the complex problems we face—from navigating our own health, work, and relationships to dealing with social unrest and global crises. In fact, I believe the noise in our minds and our inability to tend to it is one of the most under-addressed, underdiagnosed, under-named threats to the health of ourselves and our relationships, including our relationship with God.

We lack the spaciousness, the quiet, and the tools to sort through a mind—and a world—that can feel overwhelming and even frightening to us. Instead of working our way through the turmoil inside, we trudge along the same well-worn path we've traveled in the past, hoping things will be different.

And when nothing changes, we turn to the ultimate self-sabotaging strategy: we guilt-message ourselves with a stream of negative self-talk.

You just need to get it together! You shouldn't be so sensitive.

You shouldn't feel this way! You should be grateful for what you have.

What's wrong with you? You shouldn't be selfish!

Each guilt message has a grain of truth in it, which is what makes it so powerful. Of course we don't want to feel angry, even when our trust has been broken. Of course we want to feel grateful, even though we secretly wrestle with feelings of hurt or sadness. Of course we don't want to be selfish or stingy, even though we've given and given and gotten nothing in return.

And so we become masters of beating ourselves up. We have a guilt message for everything, even the fact that we know we shouldn't guilt-message ourselves! But what we don't realize is that guilting, berating, or shaming ourselves into silence only stirs up more noise inside. It adds more chaos to a situation that's already confusing. It doesn't help us find a way out of the chaos and into the conviction we need to take charge of our lives.

We replay the loop of guilt messages in our minds until we're exhausted. And in the face of exhaustion, the noise in our minds intensifies. We continue to move forward amidst the swirling truth-splinters, doing exactly what we've been doing up until this point. We avoid, procrastinate, self-criticize, or self-gaslight, and then, of course, we numb.

Reach for the phone.

Reach for the chips.

Reach for someone else's problems to fix.

We do whatever it takes to drown out the cacophony of our own inner turmoil. And we end up making things worse.

We blow past an opportunity to fight for something beautiful with a nod and a half-hearted "I wish it could be different."

Does this sound familiar to you? When we don't stop and face the chaos in our minds, we stay stuck. We sabotage our dreams. We feel resentful of others and mad at ourselves. We stay frustrated with God for not solving our problems, and then we bombard ourselves with even more guilt messages: *I shouldn't feel this angry, mixed-up, or confused! I shouldn't feel so exhausted and overwhelmed! I shouldn't feel this way about myself, my loved one, my life!*

But, dear reader, you do feel this way. All of us do at times.

Reaching a Crossroads

Life is complex. Your challenges are complex. Your mind is complex. On any given day the average person processes about eleven million bits of information per second[1] and anywhere from six thousand to seventy thousand thoughts.[2] You experience emotions during at least 90 percent of your day, often several emotions simultaneously. What's even more astonishing is that the majority of that information, including your thoughts and feelings, is processed outside your conscious awareness.[3]

You can learn to navigate your way through that complexity. Or you can operate your mind as if it were a self-driving car. You can sit back and ignore it, letting it drive. You can cruise through your day on autopilot, hoping that the car has been programmed correctly. The problem is, What if it's not? What if the car is speeding you through busy intersections or taking you down roads you have no business being on? What if it's putting you in danger, because you haven't yet learned how to avoid obstacles or take necessary detours?

You've assumed that you're heading in the right direction. But the conflict you feel inside is making you wonder if you need to change course. You're confused. You have no clue how to shift gears, let alone how to change directions. You're not sure what to do. And so you keep moving ahead, trying to tell yourself to stop feeling the way you feel.

It doesn't work.

What if that swirl of inner turmoil—the frustration, the longing, the confusion, and even the guilt—is a signal for you to stop?

The truth is you *shouldn't* feel that angry or resentful all the time. You *shouldn't* feel that worried or scared or numb. You *shouldn't* feel that conflicted or ashamed. But not because those feelings are your fault. Your body, your mind, and your heart all need something from you. Not just a rest or a break or a pep talk, though all of those can be helpful. You need to be shown a way to untie the knots. A way to quiet the noise inside. A way to navigate through the complexity. A way to take charge of your life.

Change starts when you finally stop beating yourself up for the way that you feel and say, "You know what? I *do* feel this way!"

Suddenly the spinning, guilt-messaging part of your brain screeches to a halt. It stops racing down its familiar blazed pathway of "But this is how I've always done it"—the road that leads straight to self-sabotage.

And so you choose to stop.

You see you're at a Crossroads. There are a lot of possibilities here. You're not sure how to make sense of it. You feel disoriented at first. But you choose to take a deep breath, get out of the car, and look around.

You notice that it's quieter here at the Crossroads. No noise. No guilt messages. No memes. Just questions.

Why am *I so tired and run-down?*

Why am *I so frustrated all the time?*

What is this painful feeling all about?

What's really going on in my work or in this relationship?

You start trading the chaos in your mind for curiosity, presence, and reflection. You don't know which way to proceed yet. That's okay. You've taken the most important first step. You've stopped. You've given yourself a shot at turning the car around and finding a better direction.

It's hard to stop when you're feeling conflicted. The Crossroads can be disorienting. It makes sense that you might not want to stop and camp out where you're already confused, where you're already struggling. What good will that do? It feels better to just avoid it.

Unless things could be different.

The Big Picture

What if I could hand you a map? A guide through the maze of your mind? A way out of the chaos and into a calm, clear place from which you can navigate through challenges in your life?

The good news is this: You can learn to harness the power of your conflicting thoughts and mixed-up emotions to work for you instead of against you. You can learn to disentangle the truth from the lies all around you, including the ones inside your own mind. You can find your way out of the haze of confusion into the wholehearted life and relationships that God wants for you.

It starts when you slow yourself down.

You stop.

You get curious.

And then you move in a brave new direction.

Here's the thing: tumultuous feelings and conflicting beliefs provide powerful clues to what is happening both inside you and all around you. Each feeling or belief represents a valuable clue. When you remove the guilt and examine the clues, a strange thing happens. You begin to see the big picture—of your emotions, your reactions, your problems, your relationships, your life. But you can't get that clarity while you're moving on autopilot. You have to learn to mind your mind.

The work of minding your mind is a skill most people aren't taught. It takes awareness and attunement. It takes spaciousness and curiosity. It takes tenacity and intentionality. It takes prayer and rationality. But as you get good at it, the process of minding your own mind—of noticing and reflecting on your inner dialogue, thoughts, and emotions—becomes one of the most rewarding parts of being an image-of-God-bearing human.

Consider a puzzle composed of thousands of pieces. Each tiny piece is essential. But each tiny piece is also meaningless when it's disconnected from the whole picture. Initially, when you're putting together that puzzle, you have to work slowly, examining each piece with careful attention. What are the different shapes? Are there edges on one or both sides? Where are those corner pieces? What colors go together? You examine each piece, and you group them together. And then, as you work, you connect some of the pieces. Suddenly you see how two, three, five, seven pieces all fit together to create one tiny section of the puzzle. You start to notice the patterns. You're making progress. The picture is revealing itself to you.

Each individual piece is vital. But taken by itself, it doesn't get you very far. The same is true for your feelings and thoughts and even some of the half-baked half-truths that other people have been telling you. Each piece represents one tiny part of the whole picture. When you take the time you need to notice, observe, and organize the different fragments in your mind, a clear picture emerges— one that brings peace out of the pieces. Each individual piece snaps into place to show you a larger, fuller picture of your life and of the challenges you face. These tiny truth-pieces—when tenderly, painstakingly brought out in front of you and examined—become your guides to a way out of the chaos.

As you notice the pieces, name them, and gather them together in a meaningful way, they become your most valuable gifts—each one a truth-piece on your journey toward freedom.

I'm frustrated.
I'm not entirely ungrateful. Part of me loves the life I have.
Some things are okay.
A lot of me feels misunderstood.
Some things are hard.
I don't like feeling that way.
I do feel this way.

You slow yourself down. You take some deep breaths. You realize that, yes, this is complicated, but with a little time and attention, you can find your way through it.

As you attune to the different truth-pieces living inside you, you unleash the most powerful strategy yet: you start aligning yourself with reality.

What's really happening here?
What's true?
What's not true?
What are the obstacles?
What has to be faced that can't be changed?
What are the resources available to me?

You gaze unflinchingly at the truth. You start naming things honestly. You stop pretending. You stop trying to gaslight yourself into believing things aren't what they really are. You stop putting a whole lot of energy into manipulating yourself into feeling great. You stop trying to bury the complicated blend of love, gratitude, and resentment that exists simultaneously inside you. You stop telling yourself that you don't feel the things you actually do feel.

And a strange thing happens—instead of feeling worse, you actually feel a little bit better. You stop fighting against the reality of your experience, and instead you surrender to the process of shaping it. You start working with the whole truth, the fullness of that truth, as your greatest ally. You use all that complexity to your advantage. You see glimpses of an even more beautiful, even more expansive picture that lies ahead of you.

You start to make sense of yourself and the reality of your experience.

You start to make sense of the people around you.

You start to make sense of your life!

As you piece together the contents of your heart, soul, and mind—without guilt, shame, or criticism—you gain clarity.

CLARITY GIVES BIRTH TO ACTION.

The pieces begin to align, and you arrive at a resounding realization: *I do feel this way! And I can do something about it.*

Clarity gives birth to action.

I Do Feel This Way

I don't know what problem has stirred up a seemingly unsolvable mess of conflicting thoughts inside you. It might be the realization that someone you love—a colleague, a friend, or even your own family member—has betrayed you. It might be a long-standing habit or a coping tactic you just can't seem to let go of. It might be resentment or frustration you're feeling about yourself, a loved one, or even God.

Regardless, you have found yourself plunked down at this strange place called the Crossroads. You're confused and scared, uncertain and disoriented. You don't know exactly where you're going. Part of you wants to keep hobbling along, shackled by guilt and frustration. You wish you didn't feel this way.

But you do.

You do feel this way. You do feel racked with fear, criticism, or self-doubt. You do feel caught between guilt and resentment. You do feel unsure how to sort it all out.

It's okay. The fact that you're aware of *what* you are feeling is an important first step.

This is complicated.

Yes. It's complicated. That's true.

I don't know which path to take.

Yes. That's true too.

I don't want to feel this way.

Yes. That's also true.

I've met with thousands of travelers just like you who are confused, scared, and exhausted. You might feel ready to settle, give up, check out. Don't do it! Your life is far too precious. When Jesus described a kind of truth that sets you free, he knew what he was talking about.[4] It's not a quick fix. It's not the easy way. But I promise you that when you slow down and gently attune to your mixed-up mind, you'll discover the beauty of aligning yourself with reality. You'll piece together a fuller picture of the challenges you face. You'll stop feeling stuck and start seeing a path emerge through the haze. You'll start moving forward with conviction to create the life that you crave.

Name. Frame. Brave.

This book is your guide. It's based on a process I've used for twenty years to help thousands of people who are stuck just as you are, a process I call "Name. Frame. Brave." It's a process of noticing thoughts and feelings, reflecting on them, and then translating that work into action. This book is the first time I've articulated this process in detail. It's not based on a specific therapeutic modality, though it works in conjunction with many of them.[5] It's grounded in research. It applies to all of life, not just therapeutic situations. It doesn't promise instant gratification. But it is the best gift I can give you if you want to harness the power of your own inner conflict to create a life that is wise, beautiful, and brave.

I've boiled down the process into three simple steps:

1. Name what's hard.
2. Frame your reality.
3. Brave a new path.

The simplicity of these three steps in no way implies that the approach is a quick or magical solution. It's not. But each of these steps is a powerful guide that will set you on a path toward clarity. Naming takes command. If you skip naming you'll solve the wrong problems or you'll continue down the same old path. Framing brings perspective. If you skip framing you'll have a clear name for something but you'll apply the wrong solution to it. Braving takes action. If you skip braving you'll get a little taste of clarity but you'll never actually make a change.

All three are essential, and they are also iterative. When you stop to name, frame, and brave a challenge you face, no matter how small or big, you empower yourself to choose a wise path through it. You discover the deep-down satisfaction of facing what's true about yourself and your relationships. You learn to tame your guilt—and your fear—and discover the joy of clarity and conviction. You gather the support you need to tackle the obstacles you face, and you move from self-sabotage into brave, confident action. You assemble a life that radiates the fullness of your God-given potential.

And you discover the best kind of freedom. It's the freedom that comes from facing your life honestly and living with intention. It's the freedom of knowing you have nothing to prove and no one to blame. It's the freedom of feeling valued, fulfilled, and at peace.

TWO

Name What's Hard

"I'm done trying!" Chloe said as she entered my counseling office early on in our relationship. "This marriage isn't good for me. I'm angry all the time."

I had worked with Chloe for several weeks, and she was the last person one would describe as angry. But as we met together this particular week, a bitterness erupted from behind her bright smile, and she started to get really honest with me.

"Scott's a good dad, and our kids adore him. But I feel so angry toward him all the time. I know I shouldn't feel this way. But he gives all his attention to his work, the gym, his friends—to everyone but me. I know we can't be best friends all the time. But I just feel so tossed aside. I can't do it anymore. I'm tired of feeling this way."

As I listened to Chloe, my own conflicting thoughts piped up, each a fragment reflecting aspects of the countless stories I'd heard like this:

Gosh, relationships are hard.

But we're so quick to leave things these days.

And sometimes we need to leave things, especially when they're toxic.

But sometimes we need to persist, heal, or grow.

Also, marriage can be hard. So painful when you don't feel valued.

As a clinician and as a human, I've learned that my own flurry of conflicting thoughts is a sign that I need to gently slow down the pace of my mind. It's a signal to take a deep breath to ease the firing of my nervous system and settle into the groundedness of my body.

It's a cue that the situation in front of me is complex and that I need to pay close attention so that I don't rush into an assumption that does not adequately address the reality of what's happening. In other words, it's an invitation to spend some time hanging out at the Crossroads. In this case it meant I needed to invite Chloe to join me there before she rushed into a high-stakes pseudo solution.

And so I said to Chloe a phrase that has become my mantra these past twenty years: "Could we pause here for a moment? We need to start naming some things."

Like many of us when we experience conflicting thoughts or mixed emotions, Chloe was trying to jump right into a solution without first understanding the complexity of the problem she was facing. She hadn't yet uncovered what was underneath the resentment she was feeling. She couldn't get to a better place if she didn't first stop and name what was happening.

Start with Yourself

When we're tangled up inside, it's hard to maintain perspective. Complicated or painful situations detonate conflicting thoughts and feelings that can feel chaotic and overwhelming. Often one strong emotion is colliding with another equally strong one. You might feel anger, but then you feel guilty about feeling anger. Or you might feel hurt, but then you feel anxious about taking action. Your reactions might be related to a current experience, or they might be influenced by past events. Shame may enter in and you criticize yourself, further complicating an already complicated mix.

Your nervous system gets activated, and you tend to react based on prior conditioning or automatic responses rather than thoughtful, conscious awareness. It's incredibly challenging to respond wisely to what's happening outside of you until you acknowledge and patiently work through the turmoil inside of you. The very first step is to stop and notice what you're experiencing: Name what's hard. Start with yourself.

NAME WHAT'S HARD. START WITH YOURSELF.

Naming is a profound act of noticing, acknowledging, and validating the truth of what you're thinking and feeling at any given moment. You stop anxiously ruminating, impulsively reacting, or grasping for a solution and start paying attention to what's happening inside your own mind. *What am I feeling right now? What's happening inside?* Naming the truth of your inner experience is a powerful step toward clarity. It empowers you to make a wiser choice.

The simple act of stopping to notice what you're thinking and feeling—without criticism, judgment, or shame—brings calm to the chaos inside. You shift out of overdrive and into a neutral gear, creating a pause where you can get curious about what's happening.[1] Imagine you're at a gathering and you begin to feel overwhelmed, left out, or tempted to lash out at someone. What if, instead of berating or gaslighting yourself—instead of telling yourself you shouldn't feel that way—you took a deep breath and asked yourself, *What am I experiencing right now?*

Am I hurt? Sad? Scared?

Is someone being cruel?

God, help me understand what's happening in this moment.

Instead of reacting or overreacting to the situation in front of you, you begin to gently name the truth-pieces inside of you.

Sometimes, it's hard to figure out a name for what you're experiencing right away, especially when you're facing a complicated situation that evokes complicated thoughts and feelings. That's okay. Pausing to notice *This feels complicated* or *This feels hard* is often the very first step in naming. The most important act at this juncture is to give yourself permission to notice what you're experiencing without shame.[2]

The process of naming isn't always definitive, especially at first. It reminds me of trying to come up with a name for remote hiking trails that are off the grid in my home state of Wyoming. As my family and I discuss how to name where we're going in case of an emergency, the conversation goes a little like this: "If you head out about five miles east toward Sibley Lake, you'll see a turnout on your left. It's just before the long hill that descends toward Steamboat

Rock. Drive a little ways down that bumpy dirt road. Don't take the short road to the right—it's the longer one that forks to the left! At the bottom of it, you'll find the trailhead." It takes a few iterations to find a name sometimes!

Likewise, it takes a few tries to give inner experiences an accurate name. It means slowing yourself down, describing what's happening as honestly as you can, and identifying what you're thinking and feeling in reference to other landmarks in your life. For instance, when I asked Chloe to name what was happening inside her mind as she thought about her marriage, she paused and reflected. She then answered, "It feels so foolish—but I feel left out, completely rejected. It's like I'm in fifth grade again and no one will play with me. I *hated* feeling that way!" Her husband's behaviors—whether intentional or not—had exposed a trail leading to a painful memory inside her mind. Naming those feelings became the starting point for our journey together.

Naming is like dropping a pin on a map that labels the starting point of where you are. It requires patience and self-awareness. It means asking others to wait while you take your time to get it right: "I'm trying to name what's going on with me. I'm not sure how to say it yet." But with care and attention, you'll identify a name that not only you but other people will understand: "Aha! This is where I am!"

NAMING TOOLS

When you start to name what's hard, journal naming is one of the most helpful practices. Research shows that writing out what you're thinking and feeling increases conscious awareness, improves resilience, and decreases stress.[3] When you're facing a challenging situation, set a timer for ten to fifteen minutes and write out what you're thinking and feeling. As you write, pause to notice what it's like to connect with those thoughts and feelings. Repeat this practice over several days. Journal naming in this way brings your whole brain online—it allows you to honor raw emotions while simultaneously organizing them.[4]

You might also use a feelings wheel[5] or artistic expression, such as drawing, painting, or listening to music to find names for what you're experiencing. Parts work—the topic of my first book with Kimberly Miller, *Boundaries for Your Soul*—is a powerful way to name different parts of yourself.[6] Brené Brown's beautiful book *Atlas of the Heart* is another wonderful naming tool.[7] You might also enlist the help of a friend: "I need to do some naming work. Are you available to help me?" Regardless which tool you use, the experience of inner conflict is a cue: Name what's hard. Start with yourself.

Name the Precipitating Event

Naming starts with yourself and is then informed by the reality of your external circumstances. It involves accurately identifying the outer events that are precipitating an experience of inner conflict.

When you notice that you're activated, ask yourself, *What happened that led to this feeling?* Remember, get curious. You're working to make observations, not judge, criticize, or problem solve. Simply go back in your mind to what you were doing before you noticed the jumble of complicated feelings. What is the event or interaction that precipitated the internal turmoil? Here are some examples:

- hearing a comment from another person
- observing another couple interact in real life or in a movie
- seeing a friend's vacation pictures on social media
- receiving feedback from your boss
- interacting with other parents at your child's school
- listening to a pastor speak on a sensitive topic
- running into someone from your past
- receiving an email or text

When you stop to connect your inner experience with what is happening outside of you, you gain important clarifying information. For example, if you notice that you feel guilty or bad about yourself after spending time with someone, ask yourself what happened when you were with that person. Did they criticize or guilt-trip you? Did they ignore a bid you made for connection? Did they embarrass you? Naming what happened outside of you helps you to understand the turmoil that got kicked up inside of you. Instead of beating yourself up for feeling what you feel, you become more aware. *Something* did *happen. No wonder I feel this way.*

Sometimes, the precipitating event does not fully explain the inner conflict that you feel. For example, you might feel lonely after spending time with your closest friends. Or you might feel sad after you score a big success. That's important information. Name that too. *I'm confused by what I feel. I wonder what else is going on?* Here are some examples of recent namings I've heard from clients and friends:

- "I'm sad about losing my loved one, but I also feel relieved."
- "I'm humiliated by her behavior, even though I didn't do anything wrong!"
- "I'm anxious about getting married, even though I'm happy."

Each of these namings has different implications for the path you'll need to take.

NAMING IS THE FIRST STEP TOWARD TAKING COMMAND OF YOUR OWN DESTINY.

At this point, you're simply becoming more conscious, more aware, of your own mind and the circumstances that evoked the inner turmoil. Naming is the first step toward taking command of your own destiny.

NAMING QUESTIONS

Naming questions tend to start with "What." They encourage you to identify what you're experiencing without analyzing it or jumping to conclusions about it. When you notice an activated emotional state, ask yourself the following questions.

Name Your Experience

1. *What am I feeling?*
2. *What thoughts do I notice?*
3. *What physical sensations am I aware of in my body?*

Name the Precipitating Event

1. *What happened?*
2. *What was I doing when I started feeling this way?*
3. *What past events might have contributed to my current reaction?*

A Well-Fitting Name

Names matter. When you name something, you call it into being. You give it definition. You imbue an experience with meaning. It feels terrible when you're struggling with something such as anxiety or depression only to be told by someone else that what you're really dealing with is "sin." If you're dealing with discrimination, it's demoralizing to be told you're being too "sensitive." It's tragic when someone is labeled "abusive" when they have simply set a healthy boundary that the other person does not like. It is equally tragic when a behavior that *is* abusive does not get named appropriately and those perpetrating harm are not held accountable for their actions.

When you identify a well-fitting name for an experience, it provides profound relief. Think about when you've struggled with a medical problem or a mental-health issue. A well-fitting name helps to validate the reality of your experience: "There *is* a name for this! I'm not crazy after all!" As interpersonal neurobiologist Dr. Dan Siegel teaches in his insightful book *The Whole-Brain Child*, we have to "name it to tame it."[8] According to Siegel, "merely assigning a name or label to what we feel literally calms down the activity of the emotional circuitry in the right hemisphere [of the brain]."[9] The wonder of your design is that as you identify and name your experiences you bring order out of chaos.

NAMING EXAMPLES

Consider the following list of names and the powerful feelings they evoke:

- Abused
- Addicted
- Adjusting
- Anxious
- Burnt-out
- Content
- Depressed
- Discouraged
- Grieving
- Growing
- Hopeful
- Lonely

- Marginalized
- Numb

You know that you're onto something true and wise when the naming brings relief. It reduces inner tension. You start to gain perspective. The path ahead becomes more visible. You can convey what you've named to others, facilitating greater understanding. In short, you'll experience any of the following qualities, all of which begin with the letter *c*: calmness, clarity, curiosity, compassion, confidence, courage, creativity, or connectedness.[10]

Move Toward Each Other

Naming also paves the way for a deeper experience of intimacy. You no longer wait around hoping that others will read your mind or connect the dots of your behaviors. Instead, you can name what you're experiencing authentically. "I'm anxious. It's almost always related to thinking about my financial situation." "I'm lonely, especially on the weekends." "I'm angry. I wish I didn't feel that way, but I do." You proactively invite your loved ones to come alongside you more effectively.

MEPS CHECK-IN

One of my favorite naming tools for facilitating authentic connection is a MEPS check-in. Think of one word to describe what you're experiencing in each of these categories: mentally, emotionally, physically, and spiritually. Here are a few examples:

- **Mentally:** I'm confused.
- **Emotionally:** I'm worried.
- **Physically:** I'm rested.
- **Spiritually:** I'm struggling.

- **Mentally:** I'm focused.
- **Emotionally:** I'm lonely.
- **Physically:** I'm tense.
- **Spiritually:** I'm grateful.

- **Mentally:** I'm scattered.
- **Emotionally:** I'm happy.
- **Physically:** I'm energized.
- **Spiritually:** I'm hopeful.

You can do a MEPS check-in before any activity or conversation. For example, you might do one before a meal with your family or in the car with your kids, before a night out with a friend or spouse, or before any small group gathering.

In addition, when you've done your own naming work, you gain confidence. You can enter into challenging conversations with more resolve. As my client Chloe named the rejection she was feeling in her marriage, she realized that she needed to share with her husband some of what she was experiencing. Armed with that clarity, she named something hard out loud. "Honey, I feel left out when you make plans without telling me." Initially, he didn't understand—he launched into a defensive reply and accused her of criticizing him. She stayed calm and held her ground. "I'm not criticizing you. I need to name that this hurts me. It's important to me that I tell you, even though it's hard."

The truth of her words spoke volumes. She *wasn't* criticizing him. She wasn't activated. She didn't have an agenda. She was taking command of herself—not trying to control or change him. And her husband recognized the need to pay attention. They had a real conversation for the first time in years. The truth is that regardless of how the other person responds, naming what's hard is an act of integrity. Naming cracks open the door to the possibility of change.

Finally, one of the best parts of naming is when you get the privilege to name the good you see in other people. What I love most about my job as a therapist is helping my clients name the good that lies within them that they often cannot see: "I see a loving heart." "I don't see someone selfish. I see someone who is in pain." "I see someone who's working overtime to do her part." Naming buried goodness unlocks healing and catalyzes God-given potential.

When you name, you confront reality as it is—both what's good and what's hard. You eradicate self-deception and false guilt messages. You lay a solid foundation for deep, compassionate understanding of yourself and of other people. You foster resilience, nurture integrity, and create a life of congruence where your thoughts, feelings, and actions align harmoniously. You gain the remarkable ability to discern the truth not only about yourself but about other people.

You become a Namer.

Becoming a Namer

A Namer is a truth seeker, someone who commits unwaveringly to the process of uncovering what is true and aligning with that reality. To become a Namer is to become someone who bravely confronts yourself and the complexity of your circumstances with relentless honesty. Naming is a place of psychological and spiritual wrestling—a place where you'll need to detach from the world's deceptions and distractions. It requires the courage to face the whole of yourself, including all that's good and all that's still mending.

God is the ultimate Namer, one who names with incredible intention and tender authority. In Genesis 1 God spoke forth names, such as *light*, *darkness*, *heavens*, *land*, *seas*, *sun*, *moon*, and *stars*, simultaneously calling each one into being. As he named, he revealed his creative power, initiating a divine ordering of things. Throughout Scripture God continued to lovingly name specific people. For example, he named Abraham, which means "father of a multitude," and prompted Mary to name her baby Jesus, meaning "God saves."[11] Each name called forth the unique potential and purpose of the individual person. God also named toxicity, evil, and abuse with searing clarity.[12]

As humans made in the image of God, we are also Namers. We

name our children when they are born, bestowing on them tremendous dignity. Imagine if no one bothered to name a tiny baby—how hard it would be to move through life without a name! As Namers we assign value to our relationships, declaring meaningful roles, such as mom, dad, daughter, son, friend, husband, wife, brother, or sister. We name cities and countries and landmarks. We name amorphous thoughts and emotions, transforming them into discernible insights. Becoming a Namer means becoming someone who calls forth what is good and true and beautiful in ourselves and in other people. It also means bravely naming painful experiences, toxicity, and injustices.

To become a Namer is to recognize the power you have to shape perceptions, influence others, and define reality. It requires humility. It's something to approach with a decent amount of fear and trembling. There are many temptations, distractions, and pitfalls along the way. Sometimes it can be painful to name what's hard or face what's true. It's frightening to know we might name things incorrectly. But I promise you it's worth it. Naming is what frees us.

And that's exactly why the Enemy of all that is true and good in this world loves to keep us from naming wisely.

If you've followed my work for a while now, you know that I am not one who is quick to spiritualize problems. I believe that most of our challenges are best faced head-on with practicality and sound wisdom. But the truth is that when you start naming, you will bump up against the Enemy of your soul, who would love to keep you stuck, deceived, and distracted.

The Enemy of your soul knows how effective it is to keep you from naming honestly, from harnessing that power to unleash clarity. As C. S. Lewis so brilliantly described in *The Screwtape Letters*, the father of lies is the master con artist. He's dulled our senses and duped our minds with cheap naming counterfeits. He knows the power of a mental haze "to steal away [your] best years not in sweet sins but in a dreary flickering of the mind over it knows not what and knows not why."[13] He hates it when we start to untangle the truth about the problems we face, especially when we name them without shame. He loves to keep us stuck in guilt messages, in rationalizations, in self-deception. He loves to keep us always focused on blaming other people.

If you don't become a Namer, you will become someone who avoids, distracts, or worst-case scenario, gaslights yourself and other people. And your conflicting feelings won't go away. Instead, they will roar through your mind completely cut off from the ordering, organizing, meaning-making parts that are designed to help you navigate a life that's purposeful, clear, and brave.

"I'm so angry!" your amygdala will scream.

"There's no need to be angry," the guilt-messaging, self-criticizing part of your brain will scold. "You really shouldn't feel that way."

Your mind will remain divided; you'll be at war with yourself. You'll lash out at other people or numb yourself to try to shut out the noise. This is exactly what the Enemy of your soul wants to see happening inside you. And this is exactly what I want to empower you to fight.

When you cut yourself off from complicated emotions, you stay fragmented inside. But when you bring the gentle voice of naming into the chaos of your experience, you bring calm to your mind and to this life.

You begin to work with, instead of against, the grain of your God-made design.

You start telling yourself the truth: something happened that is hard. You wish you didn't care so much, that it didn't affect you so deeply. But you do. And it does. And naming that reality is exactly what your heart, your mind, your soul, your body—and this world— need for you to do.

You align yourself with God's Spirit as you spread out the truth-pieces in front of you. You access the power of all that's kind and good and wise and true.

You're upset. That's hard.

You're going through something.

It is really frustrating. I get it.

You're also frightened. That makes sense.

You don't like feeling this way.

That's true too.

You stop fighting with yourself. Instead, you start to calm yourself. You slow yourself down. You attune to your mind, your heart, your body. You start noticing what you think and what you feel with a holy, tender curiosity.

When you name what's hard, you paradoxically find peace inside. You become the kind of person who brings real care to yourself and to other people. And you become an oasis of clarity and calm for a world in desperate need of it.

THREE

Frame Your Reality

I started the process of writing this book with a lot of inner conflict. I was coming off an intense season of letting go—letting go of the ease with which I had approached my health for most of my life, letting go of control over a medical prognosis for a beloved family member, letting go of my illusions of invincibility. I was coming face-to-face with what the contours of my soul looked like when all the illusions and striving and longings, and even some of the hopes, were stripped away.

And here I was facing a new writing project, complete with a new deadline, which meant I had no choice but to enter into the Crossroads and start naming my conflicting feelings.

What do I even have to say? Do I have something valuable to give? Can I still do this thing I used to love to do?

Due to a significant health scare, there was a seismic shift in the way I was learning to care for my body. I felt lost without the old coping tactics that would have gotten me through some of this inner turmoil and anxiety. I found myself conflicted about my gifts and abilities and even my calling.

Two things kept me going: (1) I had a book contract and an idea that I absolutely loved, and (2) there is a part of me that will die before it will shirk responsibility to another person, in this case my publisher. So each day I'd drag my body to my computer and force myself to write. And each day I'd stare at the screen, my normally busy mind that can so swiftly crank out ideas simply refusing to budge.

In thirty years of journaling, eight years of graduate school, and seven years of writing professionally, this had never happened to me. But there it was. A blank mind. An empty page. Day after day after day.

What's happening to me? Why can't I write? Is it writer's block? Am I sabotaging myself? Is it a spiritual attack? Is it brain fog?

I wrestled, reflected, journaled, and prayed. But no matter how hard I tried, I kept landing on two conflicting truths, neither of which would yield: I wanted to write this book, and I could not get myself to write this book.

My journal entries grew longer and longer while my manuscript word count remained terrifyingly tiny. I tried every hack I could think of to catapult me into action.

I tried prayer: *God, what do you want me to say?*
Silence.
I tried parts work: *What part of me is blocking me?*
Silence.
I tried exorcism: *Away from me, Satan, in Jesus' name.*
Silence.
I tried Anne Lamott: *Just write words on the page, even if they're bad.*
Silence.

Finally, I reverted to good old-fashioned willpower. I cleared my schedule and told all my friends and family that I was not available for at least a month. Then I created a calendar with a strict writing goal for each day. *This will do the trick!* I thought.

But more time staring at my computer did not solve my problem. My inability to formulate coherent thoughts only grew worse.

One Friday morning, a few days into this new strategy and a few weeks into my writing conundrum, I cried uncle at this rigid schedule chaining me to my desk. As I stared out the window, I saw that the trees had somehow sprung into the green life of spring while I wasn't looking, and I had completely missed the transformation. A deep yearning welled up inside me.

I need to drive.

The thought wasn't new to me, though it had been a long time since I'd felt this specific yearning so dramatically. It was the exact thing I'd done since I was a teenager whenever chaos would rear up inside my mind. I would jump into my car and drive toward the mountains that loomed large to the west—trying to drown out the noise in my mind by immersing myself in a whole new reality.

I grabbed the keys to our old banged-up minivan and started to drive. Only God knew where I was headed. There were no mountains to beckon to me here in Boston. Instead, I found myself headed toward Cambridge, Massachusetts, near Harvard Square, which, although beautiful in the spring, is actually a terrible place to drive. The maze of roads and rotaries required to navigate one's way into Cambridge could make the clearest mind crazy. But I did not care. Something in me needed to get there.

After a good thirty minutes of traversing the narrow roads and watching for whizzing bicyclists, I found myself slowly pulling up in front of an apartment I'd rented nearly eighteen years earlier, after a series of panic attacks had interrupted my final semester of graduate school in Denver. It was an apartment I barely remembered.

Why am I here? I wondered as I sat in front of that apartment. But as I soaked in the vague familiarity of the hydrangea bushes, the magnolia and cherry trees, and the brick driveways, I began to feel transported out of the present and into another time in my life.

I recalled completing my last year of coursework for an intense doctoral program while working full-time and attempting to guilt-message my way out of extreme loneliness—combined with tremendous unnamed anxiety—by chaining myself to my work of helping other people. The anxiety-loneliness geyser I had tried to bury deep inside myself had finally burst forth in a series of crippling panic attacks that completely thwarted guilt's best efforts. I took a leave from my last quarter of coursework, and without the structure of school for the first time in nearly a decade, I had no clue what to do with myself.

In the midst of that reckoning, a family friend offered me two weeks in this apartment. Seizing the opportunity to get out of a terribly stuck situation, I landed at this random address on Shepard Street in Cambridge.

I spent just two weeks in that apartment, and I didn't do much during that time. I watched a lot of *Gilmore Girls*. I prepped for a summer school teaching job I had taken. I had dinner with my sister and strolled through the brick-paved sidewalks of Harvard Square, thrilled to see the exact spot where Matt Damon kissed Minnie Driver in *Good Will Hunting*.

I didn't do anything here. Why is this place so significant to me? And then it hit me.

That was the point: I hadn't *produced* anything here. But I'd wrestled with a great deal internally. I'd landed here after finally naming the crippling cocktail of anxiety and loneliness that I hadn't wanted to face. I hadn't seen myself as an anxiety-ridden person, someone harboring deep pain. But increasing turmoil had demanded I reckon with those painful realities, and something was going to have to change. I didn't quite yet know what I needed. I only knew I couldn't keep traveling down the path I was on.

And so at the Shepard Street apartment, I decompressed. I detoxed from stress. I removed as many pressures and obligations as I could. To the background noise of the lighthearted banter of Lorelai and Rory Gilmore, I let my thoughts untangle themselves. I didn't force any epiphanies. But as I slowed my pace and reduced expectations, I provided space for my mind to begin to process the past few years. Those two tender weeks in that apartment on Shepard Street gave me a soft place to land and gently reflect on what in the world had happened to me.

In that almost imperceptible space that exists between naming what's hard and braving a new life ahead, I had gifted myself *a place in between.*

And on this day eighteen years later, as I sat in my minivan facing a different reckoning, I recognized familiar patterns rearing back up in my current life—the guilt messages, the refusal to name what was hard, the attempt to chain myself to my work. I didn't yet know what I needed. I didn't understand why God had brought me back here. But I was finally ready to listen.

The Place in Between

Amid my best efforts to guilt-message myself into writing, something had led me to this hidden place that barely finds itself in my memory. Though short-lived, my time on Shepard Street was significant, both eighteen years earlier and in this moment of wrestling. That hard-to-find, hard-to-define place in between had served as a quiet but profound passageway, one that bridged the terror between where I'd been and the new destination I wasn't quite ready to find.

WHEN YOU NAME SOMETHING, YOU NEED TIME AND SPACE TO METABOLIZE IT.

When you name something, you need time and space to metabolize it. You need to fully understand how what's happening affects your heart, mind, and body. You might need to heal. You might need to prepare yourself for a change. You might need to grieve. You might need to initiate a hard conversation.

In religious studies, there is a name for such passageways: liminal places. Derived from the Latin word *limen*, which means "threshold," these are the in-between places you move through during periods of transition as you leave something behind and open yourself up to what might be ahead.

It's as if you've been hiking down a winding trail through the forest, surrounded by tall trees, where all you can see is the path directly in front of you. Suddenly you reach a clearing, a vista, where you can see for miles. You take a deep breath, pause for a moment, and soak it all in—where you've been, where you are now, and where you want to go. You look all around, and as you do, you relocate yourself from this new position before moving ahead.

A place in between can be quite noticeable, like my two weeks on Shepard Street. For example, the forty years that the Israelites spent in the wilderness was an extended place in between, where they left the bondage of slavery behind and prepared to enter into the promised land.[1] An engagement period often functions as a place in between during which each individual leaves behind a single life and adjusts to the idea of a future shared with their spouse. You might think of a pregnancy as a place in between—a period of time to adjust to taking on a new role as a mother. Some cultures honor prolonged grieving periods, such as sitting shiva, as a liminal place for those who are mourning a loss. Recovery centers provide a place in between where individuals recovering from a mental-health crisis or an addiction prepare to reenter their day-to-day lives.

A place in between can also be fairly inconspicuous. For example, it might be your commute from work to home, as you consciously leave behind the worries of the day and prepare to greet your family. It might be an afternoon walk that you take as you transition from one set of tasks to another. It might be your therapist's office, where you begin to unpack the pain from your past. It might be your morning prayer time as you prepare to greet a new day. It might be a deep breath.

Regardless of how big or small, these places in between are crucial. They're where inner transformation occurs—where you deliberately slow yourself down, consciously disrupt old impulses, attend to your emotions, notice your thoughts, and develop a more complete understanding. You provide space for yourself to reflect.

The problem is we don't normalize these in-between places, at least not in our fast-paced American culture. Instead, we're expected to move quickly to the next thing—to jump from naming a challenge to fixing it. Think about the last time you confided in someone. Maybe you finally named something hard: "My marriage isn't working. I'm struggling." Or "My health isn't good. I'm not feeling well." How did that person respond? Did they ask questions and sit with you as you explored the nature of the problem? Or did they jump to a fix? "Yep. Marriage is hard. You just have to make it work!" Or "Have you tried taking this supplement to feel better? It worked for me!" In our culture we love to leap right into fixing problems instead of helping each other pause to reflect on the many different truth-pieces of our stories.

Inhabiting a place in between requires a set of qualities and skills we're not often taught. It requires presence, focus, and tenacity to examine the truth-pieces, get to the root of a challenge, and acquire deep understanding. It requires spaciousness and attention to sift through the contents of your own mind. You see these qualities in a friend who understands that sitting with you quietly or asking gentle questions is often far more powerful than rushing in with advice. You see them in a doctor who carefully helps you understand the different options available before treating a complex medical condition. You see them in a psychologist who gently creates safety before unearthing a painful wound that's been buried for years. And you see them in a wise leader who recognizes that healing a church or a nation requires patient listening and deep understanding versus flashy proclamations.

A place in between is not necessarily the most comfortable place to be. It can be disorienting and even lonely. It can be hard to explain the value of these places to other people. They might not understand why your midday walk is precious to you or why you're not available when you're cooking or gardening or while you're drinking your morning coffee. They might not understand why you'd prefer to sit in quiet while driving in your car or why you value therapy. But *you* will understand—especially when you discover how such a place can transform your life.

The Art of Framing

A place in between helps you bridge from naming what's hard to braving a new path. It's where you do the work of framing; you develop a clearer understanding of your situation. While naming primarily involves what is happening in the present moment— *What am I feeling? What's happening?*—framing moves into deeper reflection—*How long has this been happening? Why is it happening? How do I want it to be different?* Much of the work of framing unfolds beneath the surface, deep within your heart, where it leads to greater conviction and commitment when it comes time to take action.[2] Framing is an art more than it's a science.

If you're anything like me, you might be tempted to shift into overthinking or overanalysis as you work to frame your problem, to tear into it with your left brain like a dog with a bone. (There's a reason my friends used to call me Analison.) Analysis has its place, but you can't demand deep understanding. Insight can't be forced. Revelations can't be rushed. You need left-brain analysis *and* right-brain creativity to gain perspective. Framing is a delicate balance of both. If you focus too hard on the intricacies of a challenge, your left brain will hijack you and you'll overthink or ruminate. On the other hand, if you focus too much on possibilities, you'll float off into unrealistic daydreaming or fantasy. The trick is to focus just enough on the challenge, while simultaneously opening up your mind to multiple perspectives. Your mind becomes like a telescope: homing in and expanding out, examining details and dreaming expansively.

The goal is to cultivate the right conditions in your place in between where you can unlock the creativity and insight of your God-made design. That includes engaging in calming activities and minimizing distractions as you gently place your attention onto a challenge. If you notice heightened emotions, tension, or anxiety while framing, that's a cue to slow yourself down. Take some deep breaths and apply the process of naming to what you're feeling. Remember: these steps are iterative. You have time. You do not have to rush this process. The situation is perhaps more complicated than you originally thought. Stay patient with yourself as you develop this practice. Take a break. Call a friend or take a walk. When I spent time framing my anxiety on Shepard Street, I relied on *Gilmore Girls* episodes to help me stay calm and pace myself. You might consider revisiting places that are soothing to you, rereading favorite books or listening to music or watching shows that are calming or spark your imagination in positive ways.

PLACES IN BETWEEN

When identifying a place in between, choose activities that require some level of focus but are also enjoyable. These conditions allow your mind to relax and gain clarity. Here are some examples:

- Enjoy a cup of coffee or tea in a favorite setting.
- Craft, knit, or make art.
- Hike or take a long walk.
- Take a shower or a bath.
- Take a drive.
- Garden, cook, or organize.
- Play a musical instrument or dance.
- Visit a church when no one else is there.
- Sign up for a retreat.
- Meet with a therapist or spiritual director.

Loving the Questions

In the words of beloved poet Rainer Maria Rilke, framing is a time to be "patient toward all that is unsolved in your heart and try to love the questions themselves."[3] It's a place where you ask questions, sometimes questions you can't answer right away. It's a place where you connect with the gentle whisper of God's Spirit.[4]

When you move into the work of framing a challenge, here's what you're trying to unearth: *What is the actual problem here? What's my part? What's not my part? What are the obstacles? What has to be faced that can't be changed? What are the resources available to me?*

Use the following acronym to help guide your framing process:

F—Facts: Clarify the different facts of the situation to help you gain objectivity.

R—Roots: Reflect on your deeper motives for change, as well as the deeper causes of the situation. Consider past events, such as childhood experiences.

A—Audit: Review strategies you've tried in the past and assess whether those actions have worked.

M—Mental Messages: Examine your thoughts, feelings, and attitudes, as well as the expectations you've internalized. Consider alternative ways of thinking about the situation.

E—Expansion: Expand your understanding through research, expert opinions, or conversations with trusted friends. Imagine how you'd like to feel or draw a picture to gain insight.

Take, for example, a seemingly simple problem related to household chores. You frequently come home from work and find dishes piled up on the kitchen counter. You've had it. You feel angry, and you also feel disrespected. You've named the inner conflict. What's your next move? Do you shrug it off and once again clean up the dishes yourself? Do you yell at your kids? Do you call a family meeting where you discuss shared responsibilities? Do you hire a therapist, because you cannot for the life of you figure out how to establish healthier boundaries?

Let's apply the step of framing to illustrate how you might pause before launching into action. First, identify your place in between. In this case you take a deep breath and decide to go for a walk. While on that walk, you ask yourself some of the following questions:

- **Facts:** *Who are the primary characters involved? How often does the problem occur? When did the problem start?*
- **Roots:** *Why is it important to resolve?*
- **Audit:** *What strategies have I tried in the past? What worked? What didn't work?*
- **Mental Messages:** *What guilt messages am I telling myself about this situation?*
- **Expansion:** *What are some basic principles of boundaries I could learn?*

This situation might seem simple at first glance, but you'd be surprised how easy it is to jump to a conclusion that doesn't fit the situation. You might come down hard on your kids when, in fact, your spouse is enabling them. Or you might discover that although you've been muttering under your breath about the dishes for months, you've never actually asked for help or established a healthy boundary. Taking a moment to frame your inner conflict now will spare you years of pent-up resentment in the future.

You might also ask yourself size and scope questions so that you can pace yourself and gather the appropriate level of support. *Is the size of this problem small, medium, or large?* For example, when I first encountered anxiety in graduate school, the impact was large. I couldn't sleep. I couldn't make it through a class without calling my sister in a panic. I could barely read a book. As a result, I took time off from school and enlisted the support of a therapist to help me cope with anxiety. Taking the time I needed to frame my anxiety accurately led to more effective, lasting results. Now when I feel anxious, I typically frame it as medium or small. If it's small I can take a deep breath or a walk to gain the clarity that I need. If it's medium I might call a friend for support.

When it comes to relationship challenges, one of my favorite methods of assessing size and scope is to locate certain behaviors on a spectrum. For example, in my book *The Best of You* I introduced readers to the Spectrum of Toxicity.[5] This spectrum is a framing tool I use to help my clients frame boundary violations they are experiencing with other people. To discern the level of toxicity, I ask my clients questions like these:

- **Facts:** How often does the problematic behavior occur? When does it occur?
- **Roots:** When did the toxicity start? What were the circumstances in which it developed?
- **Audit:** What strategies have you tried in the past? What worked? What didn't work?
- **Mental Messages:** What messages are you telling yourself about the situation?
- **Expansion:** What information do you need about abusive behaviors?

Finally, as you reflect on a challenge that you face, consider the cost of change. *What are the potential risks of making a change?* Facing the risks honestly will help you prepare for the path ahead. It's also wise to consider the alternative: *What's the cost if I don't make any change at all?*

Above all, dear reader, please know that you are worth this effort. Your life is precious. Whether you're facing a small problem or what feels like a giant mountain, creating a place in between to mindfully frame your situation is a gift you give to yourself.

THE LOOKING TOOL

The Looking Tool helps you understand how a problem fits into the larger story of your life. It consists of three parts: looking back, looking at today, and looking ahead.

Looking Back

- *Have I faced a similar situation in the past?*
- *What strategies did I use to address it?*
- *What worked? What didn't work?*

Looking at Today

- *On a scale from 1 to 10, how content am I with my current circumstances?*
- *What are the top two to three obstacles I face?*
- *What are two to three resources I have at my disposal?*

Looking Ahead

- *Envisioning my ideal future, what would progress look like one year, five years, or ten years from now?*
- *What decisions would I regret one year, five years, or ten years from now?*
- *What steps can I take now to align with my envisioned future?*

A Holy Reframe

A place in between is where you start to create a new story, a truer story, of what's happening in your life. You examine conflicting thoughts and feelings. You consciously reject old, myopic ways of thinking and replace them with a more honest, more beautiful, more whole, more holy perspective in partnership with God's Spirit. You create what I call a holy reframe.

Consider the story of Jacob in the Bible.[6] Jacob was all set to move his family back to his home country of Canaan to start a new life. But Jacob also had some unresolved issues from his past. As a result of his own deceptiveness, he'd deeply angered his brother, Esau, and caused a rift in their relationship. Years later he was going to have to face his brother again. It makes sense, then, that as he neared his home and a reunion with his brother, Jacob took some time by himself to reflect. He created a place in between, where he wrestled with God. You can almost feel the inner tensions inside Jacob at this point in the story: *I know I've done some things wrong. I deeply hurt my brother. I also know I've done some things right. I've honored my commitments to my new family members. I'm ashamed of my past. I also want my family to have a new life.*

Two things happened as a result of his time spent in that place in between: First, Jacob sustained an injury in the course of a wrestling match with God, perhaps a symbol of the truth that we don't always escape our challenges unscathed. Second, Jacob was given a new name, one that revealed a fuller picture of the story of his life. His original name meant "deceiver." But his new name meant "one who strives with God and prevails." This new name was a holy reframe. It accounted for all of who Jacob had become, not just who he had been. He was no longer a mere trickster, someone who strove only for his own selfish gain. He'd grown and changed. Jacob was still a man who strove after what he wanted, *and* he was also a man who showed humility, remorse, and care for other people. He was still the same person, *and* he was transformed.

Two Things Can Be True

When you lop off any portion of what is true, you wind up trying to deceive or gaslight yourself. On the other hand, when you create a place in between to account for the entirety of what's true, you align yourself with reality. Your creativity kicks in, and you start to envision a way through the challenges you face.

When you do this work, you often arrive at one of the most powerful holy reframes I've found: the reality that two seemingly contradictory experiences can exist side by side. Two things can be true.

I need more space from my kids, and *I adore my kids.*
My marriage is hard, and *I value my marriage.*
I'm angry with my parents, and *I want to be a good daughter.*
I want to trust God, and *I don't always trust God.*
I feel broken, and *I've never felt more whole.*

This is the bigger frame I finally discovered as I wrestled with myself and with God about this manuscript. During that struggle I came face-to-face with a recurring narrative I had used to guilt-message myself in the past: *You should work harder. You shouldn't feel anxious. You should be more disciplined.*

But that framing wasn't helpful, nor had it ever been. As I built a larger frame for my experience in light of what my mind, heart, and body needed, I understood it more like this: *I can work hard, and I can take breaks. I can feel anxious, and I can care for myself. I need discipline, and I need rest and play.*

The truth is I really wanted to do this project. I wanted to do it so much that my left brain almost sabotaged me. I hadn't factored in the reality that this new project was coming on the heels of another massive project. I had already expended a lot of energy without giving myself much time to recover. My family had also gone through a challenging season as we faced a terrifying medical diagnosis. Though it had been resolved in a positive way, I was emotionally exhausted. Parts of me needed time to recalibrate—to process all that had happened. I had moved directly from something hard into tackling a brand-new project. My body wasn't quite ready yet. I needed a place in between.

And so that's what this project became. Instead of muscling my way through the way I had done in the past, I developed a bigger frame—one that honored my desire to produce good work *and* my need to rest and recover.

I built in days dedicated to exploration and adventure. I took a good long walk with a friend to enjoy the glorious spring I had been missing. I asked my husband to go whale-watching with me! I started allowing the part of me that had been checking out while staring at my screen to take drives on a whim or to reach for a book that was calling out to me. And as I did those things, my creativity started to return. I began to make progress on my writing. Even more importantly, I had something of value to say.

Brave actions flow from clear minds.

Clear minds require places in between to honor all the truth-pieces of what you're experiencing.

BRAVE ACTIONS FLOW FROM CLEAR MINDS.

As you thoughtfully examine old ways, something beautiful happens. You gain perspective. You unlock old traps that have kept you stuck in the past—in past ways of thinking, coping, and surviving that simply do not serve you anymore. You start to see yourself in new ways, and you gain more insight into how God and others see you too. You gather confidence, and as a result you begin to brave exhilarating new paths.

FOUR

Brave a New Path

Priya loved her mom. They'd been through a lot together and in many ways had been more like best friends than mother and daughter. When Priya was thirteen, her mom had finally left an abusive spouse—and years of turmoil—behind her. Mother and daughter had become inseparable, and Priya was thrilled to rediscover a mom who was finally available to her. But over time Priya noticed that her mom's love had strings attached to it. When Priya left home and started to forge her own life, including marrying and having kids of her own, her mom seemed to resent it.

"I don't know what to do," Priya told me one day over Zoom. "I mean, I love my mom. She's incredibly tough, and she's taught me so much. On the other hand, I can't stand how controlling she's become. I find myself hiding so much of my life from her, including other friendships. She gets so passive-aggressive if I can't spend time with her. I don't want to deal with her criticism. But then I feel terrible about lying to her. It's just such an impossible situation."

As Priya laid out all the different truth-pieces of what she was feeling, a picture of a complex situation emerged: Priya loved her mom and felt loyal to her. Her mom was exhibiting some problematic behaviors. Priya was frustrated and angry with her mom. She was also lying to avoid conflict.

Priya was trapped between frustration on one side and loyalty on the other. She was grateful for her mom's good qualities. She didn't think her mom was a bad person. But she also didn't like how her mom would try to control her through passive-aggressive remarks and criticism. She didn't like feeling guilty for having a life apart from her mom. And she really didn't like lying about it.

As Priya named her conflicting feelings, we began to frame the situation using the Spectrum of Toxicity. Priya didn't think her mom was toxic. Instead, it seemed clear that while she had some good qualities, she also had some unhealthy ways of coping with her own loneliness and regrets. To move out from the conflict inside her mind and into the possibility of changing the situation, Priya was going to have to brave taking action. The question became, What was the next right step to take?

Fight, Leave, or Suffer Wisely

You've named a problem. You've framed it from every angle. You've gained clarity and deep understanding. The worst of the mental chaos is behind you. But the work is not over yet. Now it's time to take a brave step into action. It's time to initiate the change you've worked so hard to name and frame.

When it comes to braving complicated situations, I've found one of the most helpful frameworks to guide your next steps is to consider the following three options:

1. fight for it,
2. leave it, or
3. suffer it wisely.

Your first option is to fight for change. You might fight for something within yourself. For example, you might fight for improved mental or physical health or better coping strategies. You might fight for healthier boundaries. Or you might fight for a healthier relationship with someone else—a friend, parent, child, or spouse. You might fight for a job or for a dream. You might fight for justice in the world around you. You might fight for the health of your faith community.

Alternatively, through the process of naming and framing, you might determine that the best course of action is to leave something or someone behind. It may be that you need to leave behind a way of thinking, a habit, or a coping tactic that's not serving you anymore. You might need to leave a relationship that's causing harm. It's simply not wise or sustainable to continue to give this person access to you. You might need to leave a job, a church, or a group.

Finally, in many cases you'll choose the third option: to suffer wisely. Sometimes this choice is made for you. For example, you might need to suffer a health condition or a painful medical diagnosis. You can't make it go away, but you can take brave steps each day to care for yourself. You might have to suffer a job that you don't like but need. Or you might have to suffer a challenging relationship. For example, maybe you have to co-parent with an ex who betrayed you. You can't remove yourself from the hurt entirely, but you can work to mitigate further injury.

There are also times when you deliberately choose a challenging path. Having identified and understood the circumstances at hand, you might decide to remain in a challenging situation for specific, clear reasons. For example, you might choose to stay in a marriage or a relationship that's hard but not bad enough to leave. You might not sever ties with an adult child who is mistreating you, even as you set boundaries to protect yourself. You might choose to care for ailing parents even as you work to shield yourself from their criticism or guilt-tripping.

To brave the path of suffering—regardless of the cause—is a nuanced and complex act. It's a path we will all face at various times in our lives. Suffering wisely isn't passive. It requires healthy boundaries, self-care, and a skill psychologists call "radical acceptance."[1] Radical acceptance doesn't mean you approve of a situation or believe it should continue, nor does it mean you're resigning yourself to a life of misery. It's not martyring, nor is it pretending something isn't hard. Instead, it means equipping yourself to deal with a hard situation realistically—taking charge of what you can while releasing what's out of your control.

Whether you choose to fight for change, leave, or suffer wisely, you give yourself the gift of agency. Your actions flow from a place of self-awareness, inner conviction, and integrity. While you can't remove all suffering, you can wisely brave your way through it, empowering yourself to navigate challenges with resilience and grace.

One Brave Step at a Time

Braving a new path is vulnerable. As a therapist, and as a human, I love the work of naming and framing. It's often the most intuitive part of my work. But if we don't take all that insight and catapult ourselves into brave action, we're merely spectators in our own lives, missing the chance to shape our future and create real impact. To create change you have to step out of the abstract part of your mind and into the concrete world of action. You have to trust the work you've done and then take the leap.

The good news is that you take the leap one brave step at a time. Each brave step reveals the next one, and you can always course correct. You may decide to fight for change and initiate a conversation with a friend, only to discover that she gets increasingly toxic. If that happens, it's okay. That step led you to valuable information. Name what happened, **EACH BRAVE STEP REVEALS THE NEXT ONE.** frame it, then pivot and brave a different direction. Or you may decide to leave a situation, only to find that the other person seems to be more open to change than you originally thought. In that case you might choose to pivot and work to salvage the relationship instead.

For example, a former client decided to call it off with a romantic interest she had been dating for several months. As she described to him her reasons for ending the relationship, he was surprisingly attentive and self-reflective. He honored her concerns, meeting her with kindness and respect. Instead of breaking up, they had a deep conversation and found themselves working through conflict in a way that neither of them had experienced before. She took a brave step to leave, and that step led her to discover that this was, in fact, a relationship she wanted to keep. (They eventually married.) When you take one brave step in a clear direction, continue to name and frame as you move. Stay alert and attentive as you engage with each new truth-piece you encounter.

BRAVING A STEP

The acronym BRAVE can help you think of brave steps you might take. Consider different options in each of the following categories. I've given you some examples of what taking a brave step might look like.

B—Boundaries: Set clear limits to ensure your well-being.
- Set external boundaries with a toxic behavior.
- Set internal boundaries with a negative thought or attitude.

R—Range: Increase your repertoire of strategies for coping and self-soothing.
- Learn grounding exercises to calm your nervous system.
- Create a list of who is in your support system.

A—Assertiveness: Assert your preference or strengthen your voice.
- Ask for something that you need.
- Take a self-defense class.

V—Vitality: Engage in activities that are life-giving.

- ⊚ Pick up a new hobby.
- ⊚ Celebrate a milestone or success.

E—Environment: Change the environment around you.

- ⊚ Choose a new gym or coffee shop.
- ⊚ Leave a home, church, or work environment.

Braving is concrete and practical, and it's incredibly case specific. We'll explore numerous tips and scripts for how to take braving steps in parts 2 and 3 of this book. For now, I want to highlight some of the obstacles to braving that frequently trip people up when they head down a new path. Arming yourself with knowledge is a brave step in and of itself. When you anticipate the obstacles you will face, they lose their power.

The Fog of Ambivalence

One of the biggest obstacles to braving is ambivalence. The prefix *ambi-* means "both," and the suffix *-valenx* means "power." In other words, when you're ambivalent about taking action, it's typically because *both* paths in front of you have power. As a result, you feel pulled in two different directions.[2] For example, you might want to fight for change, but you can't figure out the best way forward. You switch back and forth between competing thoughts.

I need to set healthier boundaries with this person. But they're in a tough spot, and I'm concerned about hurting them.

I need to advocate for myself in this unfair situation at work. But I'm scared that if I push too hard, I could lose my job.

I need to start exercising. But I can't take time away from my demanding job, my kids, or sleep.

The presence of ambivalence doesn't mean that you don't care. (That's indifference.) Instead, ambivalence means you have weighed your options and can see both sides of a situation, making it almost impossible to make a decision. Ambivalence is an important signal to notice. It indicates the presence of legitimate complexity—that some solutions aren't obvious. If you don't name, frame, and brave ambivalence, it can operate like one of those noise machines that help you fall asleep—it creates an alternate noise in your mind that can lull you into entropy. In the midst of its white noise, you choose the path of least resistance, the well-blazed trail of whatever coping strategy you've used in the past.

If you struggle with ambivalence, don't be discouraged. Name it for what it is. Research shows that people who experience greater ambivalence tend to be less impulsive, read other people's emotions more accurately, are more creative, and tend to be fair and balanced in their evaluations of other people and situations.[3] These are great qualities that you don't want to lose! It's also true that these qualities can make it hard to take the brave action steps you need to take. F. Scott Fitzgerald summarized ambivalence brilliantly: "The test of a first-rate intelligence is the ability to hold two opposed ideas in the mind at the same time, *and still retain the ability to function.*"[4]

One of the best ways to conquer ambivalence is to give yourself a deadline. Research shows that the discomfort of ambivalence increases as you near a deadline.[5] As a result of that discomfort, you'll be forced to make a choice. Use the ambivalence chart below to frame the different aspects of your situation. Then take one brave step in a new direction by the deadline you have chosen. Remember: the goal of braving is not perfection; the goal is movement. That's the beauty of this work! Each brave step leads to more insight.

NAME, FRAME, AND BRAVE AMBIVALENCE

One of my favorite exercises to work through ambivalence is to weigh the pros and cons of each option against the cost of change.[6] Here's a step-by-step guide:

1. Name one or two options that are causing ambivalence in your decision-making process.
2. Frame the pros and cons of each option by filling in the following chart.[7]

	PROS	CONS
Option 1		
Option 2		
No Change		

3. Circle the box that carries the most weight for you.
4. Identify one brave step you can take based on the box you circled.

Brave Your Regret

As you brave a new path, you may also run into a different obstacle, the feeling of regret. Regret's voice shows up a little like this: *Why didn't I figure this out sooner? Why did I waste all that time? Why didn't I know better?*

When you make a change, you often stir up old wounds that remind you of past mistakes or regrets. This is a normal part of growth. The trick is to honor feelings of regret even as you don't let them hinder the progress you are making.

My client Ava taught me a powerful lesson about regret in my early work as a therapist. By the age of thirty-eight, she had already weathered more than her fair share of storms. A pattern of abusive relationships, stemming from unaddressed childhood trauma, had cast a shadow over much of her adult life. Two years prior to starting therapy with me, she'd managed to finally break free from the latest cycle of physical and emotional abuse. She'd sworn off men, stopped at a Crossroads, set up a place in between for herself, and embarked on a journey to heal. In many ways, she was doing great, but she was also living in isolation.

One day, as we sat in my office together, Ava told me that she had run into a childhood boyfriend, Tom, a kindhearted guy who had loved her through her tumultuous teen years. They had dated briefly, but mostly he had been her best friend. Seeing him again years later stirred up a cauldron of emotions, and she became filled with regret.

"Why was I so stupid?" she said to me, angry with herself. "He's such a great man now and a wonderful husband and dad. Why did I walk away from him? That could have been my life!"

As I listened to Ava, I fought against all the things I wanted to say to comfort her or to make the pain of regret go away. Instead, I sat with her quietly, feeling the pain with her. After a few moments I asked, "Ava, is it Tom you want, or are you longing for something he represents?"

She reflected for a moment. "It's not Tom. I'm happy for him and the life he's found. I'm just so sad about the girl I was back then. The girl he saw in me. The girl I lost shortly after we broke up."

"What was she like, Ava?" I asked.

"She was smart, good-hearted, full of life. She had dreams, so much promise and potential. And he saw that in me—he saw the woman I could have been."

"What if that woman he saw *is* you?" I asked. "What if she's still in there?"

She nodded thoughtfully, then said softly, "I want that to be true."

She told me later that something profound lifted from her that day as she named and framed her regret. She'd bravely gotten herself out of a toxic pattern of relationships. She was in a better place. But she was hesitant to brave the next leg of her journey—developing her talents and potential and even opening up to the possibility of a healthy, loving partnership. Some part of her was whispering, "It's too late for you."

When she faced regret head-on and worked her way through it, she was able to reframe that old message. While she couldn't go back in time, she could brave a new life ahead. Ava realized something incredibly powerful about the subtle nature of regret. She didn't regret that path not taken way back then. She regretted the person she hadn't yet become—and it was not too late for that!

Ava began to bravely fight for herself and for her future. She fought to change her beliefs about her potential. She braved a new job at a local art museum, a place she'd always dreamed of working. A few months later she met a man who also worked there. She braved a first date with him. Then she braved a second one. Each step along the way, she named and framed the fear or regret that would come up. Step-by-step, she braved her way into a flourishing new life and a healthy new relationship, transforming her life in ways she had once not thought possible.

Brave Your Guilt

There is one more obstacle we have to discuss. The most ubiquitous obstacle most of my clients face when they start to brave a change is guilt. When you make a change that's wise for you, it often means disappointing someone else. Guilt messages swoop in. If you're not careful, these messages will lure you back to that place of confusion and turmoil, back to where you were before you entered the Crossroads, right back to where you started: *I shouldn't feel this way!*

But you know better now.

You've done the work. You've faced what's hard. You've counted the cost of change. You've also counted the cost of *not* changing. Guilt doesn't have to trip you up. In fact, once named and tamed, you can turn guilt into a powerful new friend.

Remember my client Priya from the beginning of this chapter? As she considered braving options with her mom, she decided to fight for change. She felt she owed it to her mom to directly confront the problematic behaviors, since she hadn't spoken up about her concerns before. There was one problem: she felt incredibly guilty about establishing healthier boundaries.

Like many people, Priya was stuck in the empathy trap.[8] She didn't like what her mom was doing. She also hated the thought of bringing up potential conflict. She couldn't bear the thought of causing pain—even though her mom was the one who was misbehaving. So we created the following holy reframe: *I can set boundaries with my mom,* and *I can show her that I care.*

Priya's braving plan addressed all the truth-pieces simultaneously. She bravely named her new limits and began to shut down conversations that turned passive-aggressive or critical. "Mom, I'm not going there with you. I'm getting off the phone now." At the same time she proactively identified and affirmed their interactions that were life-giving. "I love it when you join us for dinner, Mom. We'll see you Friday!" Sure enough, Priya felt guilt the first few times she made good on her boundaries with her mother's criticism. But she didn't apologize or backtrack. Instead, she stuck to her plan and enjoyed their next Friday dinner. Anticipating guilt helped her create a stronger plan of action.

The bottom line is this: The presence of guilty feelings does not mean you have done something wrong. It might mean you have done something brave.

Guilt is an emotion, not necessarily a direct message from God. Therefore, braving guilt involves getting curious

> **THE PRESENCE OF GUILTY FEELINGS DOES NOT MEAN YOU HAVE DONE SOMETHING WRONG. IT MIGHT MEAN YOU HAVE DONE SOMETHING BRAVE.**

about it, just as you would any other feeling, such as sadness, anger, or fear. Guilt has important information for you, but it does not always have the full story.

It's helpful to distinguish between true guilt and false guilt. The messages of true guilt show up after you do something wrong. You'll know it's true guilt if you can name the thing you did wrong. *I yelled at my kids. I lied to a friend. I betrayed someone's trust—I shared their confidential information in a moment of gossip.*

In such cases, true guilt brings conviction. It involves a clear prick of the conscience, followed by clarity about the offense. You'll then need to determine your next braving steps; you'll work to change your own behaviors and apologize or make amends.

The messages of false guilt, on the other hand, show up when you haven't done anything wrong. You'll know it's false guilt if you can't name an actual thing that you did wrong. You feel a vague sense of not measuring up to some impossible standard either you or someone else has set. *I feel guilty that they feel disappointed. I feel guilty that I'm not available to my kids 24-7. I feel guilty that other people are suffering.*

In the case of false guilt, you can tell yourself a thousand different ways that you *shouldn't* feel guilty. But you do. Guilt clings to you like a frightened child. *What if I've done something wrong? What if I've hurt someone? What if I've made a mistake?* The solution isn't to try to shoo guilt away. It's to gently reframe guilt and give it a new name—one that more accurately describes what you're feeling.

The truth is that false guilt often protects you from facing other more vulnerable emotions, such as sadness, fear, and even helplessness. These emotions can be challenging to face. *I'm sad that I'm disappointing my friend. I'm worried I'm letting my kids down. I feel helpless that I can't improve their situation.*

In this case guilt is a misnaming. Of course you don't want other people to feel disappointed or let down. You don't want others to be hurting. But it's not helpful to tell yourself that these things are exclusively your responsibility.

When you experience false guilt, you essentially feel guilty for being human. You feel guilty that you're finite. You feel guilty that you're not omnipotent, omniscient, and omnipresent.

In other words, you feel guilty that you're not God.

The good news is—you're not. You're finite. You're limited. You're human. We all are.

The antidote to guilt in this case is radical acceptance of your human limitations. It's what we mean by the word *surrender*. When you surrender, you reframe your expectations of yourself.

Guilt says, "I'm letting people down," but surrender says, "I am limited, *and* I am a beloved child of God."

Guilt says, "I should be perfect," but surrender says, "I'm not perfect, *and* God's grace is enough."

Guilt says, "I should have done more," but surrender says, "I gave my best, *and* I have to trust God with the rest."

Do you see what I'm getting at? The antidote to guilt is a radical acceptance of your dependence on God. It's choosing to bravely suffer the reality of your human limitations wisely.

God, I don't want to disappoint this other person. I don't want to make a mistake. I don't want other people to suffer, and I have to be brave. I have to make decisions. I have to live within the limits of my own humanity.

Braving radical acceptance *and* radical dependence on the One who actually holds all things together is the exact opposite of the toxic positivity, half-baked half-truths, and spiritual platitudes that keep you stuck. It's the ultimate sign of an active, not passive, faith.

NAME, FRAME, AND BRAVE GUILT

When guilt messages crowd your mind, name, frame, and brave your way to clear action steps.

Name: What exactly do you feel guilty about?

Frame: Ask yourself the following framing questions.

- *Did I do something wrong? Would an objective third party agree that I did something wrong?* (If you aren't sure, ask someone.)
- *Did I hurt someone else as a result of cruelty, impatience, selfishness, or anger?* (If so, you are likely feeling true guilt.)
- *Did I hurt someone else as a result of setting a healthy boundary or honoring my human limitations?* (If so, you are likely feeling false guilt.)

Brave: Identify an action step.

- If you've identified true guilt, apologize to the person you hurt, make amends, or commit to growth.
- If you've identified false guilt, identify one fact that counters the guilt message. For example
  - *I'm not giving my kids enough attention* **becomes**

I spend twenty minutes of quality time with my kids each night before bed.

- *I'm not helping out enough at church* **becomes** *I volunteer once a month.*
- *I'm not taking care of myself* **becomes** *I take a walk each day.*

An Active Faith

To name, frame, and brave your way through life is the work of an active faith. It isn't shrugging your shoulders in the face of complexity and saying, "God's in control." An active faith means taking steps to change what you can change. It means taking responsibility for what's yours to work out. It also means bravely surrendering to the reality that you are not ultimately in power.

There's a profound shift that happens when we surrender, when we glimpse the end of ourselves and reach the boundaries of our own capacity. A moment of surrender is quite possibly the bravest act there is. It's not that challenges magically resolve themselves. It's that when we become aware of our own frailties, our own finitude, we discover that's where God loves to enter in. It's where we stumble upon a deeper strength, one that does not come from inside us, yet one that paradoxically amplifies our potential to make an even more significant change.

Surrender doesn't mean passivity. It doesn't indicate a lack of effort, nor is it giving up. You're doing everything in your power, yet these problems are just so big at times. You've reflected, and you've wrestled. You've taken courageous steps forward. In a moment of surrender all that mental work comes to a grinding halt.

You stop.

You breathe.

You release your grip.

And in that moment something clicks together.

Our loving God, who has been there all along, breaks through a little bit. That divide between where you are and where God is disappears. Your mind calms. Something inside your body shifts. You take a break. Move your body. Call a friend. You let the tears flow freely, and sometimes you sob.

And then you get back up. And with God's help you take that next one brave step.

PART TWO

I Shouldn't Feel This Way About Myself

FIVE

I Shouldn't Feel Stuck in My Head

Through all my encounters with the human psyche, there is one thing I know for sure: Our minds can be used brilliantly to solve the challenges we face. And those same minds can be used brilliantly to keep us trapped, stuck, and duped into self-sabotage. Each of us has a mind that is exceptional at playing tricks on us.

I've seen it in myself, and I see it in my clients. Sheila was no exception.

Sheila thought she was unlucky. But that would be a misnaming. Let me explain. A single woman in her early thirties, Sheila had come to see me because she was sick of feeling stuck in her head, as if she were spinning in circles and going nowhere in her life. She was struggling to pay her rent, and her student loans were mounting. She hated her job but couldn't figure out how to find another one. She was also lonely, and her dating life was nonexistent.

Sheila was hardworking and responsible. She was well educated, loved by her tight-knit family, and had a lot of close friends. She seemed to have many things going for her. Yet the moment she entered my office, she would almost immediately dissolve into tears, blurting out a flurry of self-sabotaging statements: "My life is a disaster!" "I work so hard, but things just never go my way." "I don't seem to be lucky the way other people are."

As I listened to Sheila, my mind struggled to make sense of the conflicting truth-pieces spilling out of her. She had done well in school, yet she wasn't working in her field. She expressed that she wanted a boyfriend, even though she wasn't interested in dating. She felt stuck and depressed, yet she didn't want to make any changes.

Her ability to explain away the incongruence in her life as "unlucky" was striking. So striking that it prompted me to name *that* during one of our early sessions: "I know you're struggling financially. And I know you long for a romantic partner. Those are very real things. I also sense that there's a gap inside you we haven't yet been able to name—a gap between what you really want out of your life and the decisions you are making."

The incongruence I sensed in Sheila is incredibly common. Most of us are adept at rationalizing decision-making that doesn't correlate with the life we actually want. I also knew Sheila, like most of us, might not like me putting my finger on it.

Sure enough, as she told me later, Sheila initially didn't like that naming. In fact, she left that session somewhat angry with me. *How dare she question the decisions I am making?* she fumed.

But a part of her was curious.

The truth is that something wasn't adding up in her life. When

I named that incongruence, a longing opened up inside her and she entered into the Crossroads with me. Together we started to frame the decisions she'd been making.

Why had she gone into debt to get all that education? Was she really content never to use it?

Why did she get so defensive when people asked her about what she did for a living?

What was her aversion to dating, even though she longed for a partner?

Sheila had created a story that justified certain decisions. But when she laid out all the truth-pieces honestly, the story didn't hold up. There was a tiny but crucial missing piece that we would need to uncover before she could move toward a truer, more complete picture of the life she so desperately longed to live.

When Two Things Don't Add Up

In psychology the term *cognitive dissonance* is used to describe the discomfort or tension that arises when you hold conflicting beliefs or when what you value or believe doesn't line up with your actions.[1] The term *dissonance* comes from the world of music, where it refers to a lack of harmony between musical notes. Like the clash of two notes that simply do not go together, dissonance creates an uncomfortable tension inside your mind. If you don't name and frame that dissonance, you tend to loop between the clashing thoughts without getting anywhere.

In general we don't like that feeling of dissonance. We don't like how it feels when what we believe or desire doesn't line up with how we are behaving. A wealthy rock star might feel dissonance if he constantly flies around in his private jet even as he advocates against the dangers of climate change. Or a pastor might feel it if he preaches regularly about fidelity, yet he's cheating on his wife in secret. More commonly, we experience dissonance in subtler ways. For example, you might feel uncomfortable if you enjoy time with a friend one day, only to gossip about her behind her back the next. Or maybe you pride yourself on being an ethical person, but then you find yourself lying to your spouse. It can also show up in complicated relational dynamics. You might find yourself in a toxic relationship even though you believe in your heart that you deserve better. We all wrestle with lining up our actions with our better selves. The problem isn't that we experience dissonance. The problem is when we refuse to wrestle with it.

When you notice dissonance inside you, you have two choices. Your first option is to name it, allowing the discomfort to help you align your desires, beliefs, and behaviors in a more harmonious way. You start by naming the different truth-pieces that are cre-

> **THE PROBLEM ISN'T THAT WE EXPERIENCE DISSONANCE. THE PROBLEM IS WHEN WE REFUSE TO WRESTLE WITH IT.**

ating dissonance. Remember: naming is the work of being relentlessly honest with yourself without shame. If you notice yourself lying to your spouse, name what's happening honestly: *I just lied to my husband. I don't like lying to my husband. I think it's wrong to lie.* Or if you're struggling in a toxic relationship, you might lay out your conflicting feelings: *I don't like being treated this way. I also have a lot invested in this person. I can't find it in me to just walk away.* As you name the dissonance honestly, you set yourself up to frame the situation and eventually brave a healthier path.

Your second option is refusing to name the inner tension. If you don't consciously face the discomfort of dissonance, you open the door for your mind to start playing tricks on you. A meaning-making part of you will jump in to reduce the inner tension. You might start to rationalize, defend, or justify the incongruence: *If I didn't lie, he'd get his feelings hurt!* Or *It's just gossip! Who does it really hurt?* Your mind can also start creating elaborate justifications that keep you trapped in unhealthy situations: *The way he treats me isn't really that bad. I'm tough. I can handle it!* You start creating a storyline that justifies the discrepancy between what you know to be true and your behaviors that don't quite match up to that truth.

Please hear me say this: The discomfort of dissonance is a gift! It's a cue that something in your life is out of alignment. You can name it and work through it, leading to growth and transformation. But if you ignore it or dismiss it, your mind grows chaotic—it's the opposite of mental clarity. You'll wind up stuck in a thinking trap.

Recognizing and Naming Thinking Traps

Often some of the very first—and most important—things you will need to name at a Crossroads are the thinking traps that exist inside your mind. It's almost impossible to tackle the problems you face until you first take inventory of the messages you tell yourself about them. Remember: brave actions flow from clear minds.

One of the most common signs you're caught in a thinking trap is defensiveness.[2] You form a skewed perception of yourself, others, or a situation. As a result, you might feel easily misunderstood, threatened, or criticized. You're more vulnerable to the perceptions of other people. When someone exposes an area that you feel tender about for whatever reason, a flurry of emotions kicks up. You feel guilt, fear, or shame. Suddenly your mind is poised and ready to defend you at all costs. It's how Sheila responded when I first put my finger on the dissonance in her life.

WE GET DEFENSIVE WITH OTHERS WHEN WE FEEL AT ODDS WITH OURSELVES.

How dare you question my decisions! We get defensive with others when we feel at odds with ourselves.

For example, if your boss notes that you're frequently late, you might get defensive, saying, "Why are you always singling me out? Other people are late!" You haven't confronted the truth of your behaviors, leaving yourself unequipped to engage with constructive feedback.

On the other hand, when you name and frame your inner tensions, you grow in self-awareness. You make peace with yourself, leading to more confidence with other people. When you've faced your own propensity to be late, you're able to respond in a more constructive way. "You're right," you might say. "And I know that's annoying. I'm working on it." You've taken responsibility for your own actions. You're free to accept or reject other people's opinions. Their perceptions lose power over you.

To be clear, if someone's attacking you with cruel intent, it's normal to feel defensive. Abusive people work to provoke defensiveness in you; they seek out your areas of vulnerability. They also feed on your reactions. This is not your fault! In cases of toxicity, it's wise to work with a trained professional to neutralize the impact of such attacks and extract yourself from such relationships.

Regardless of the other person's motive, defensiveness is almost always an opportunity to do some naming work inside yourself. *I'm getting defensive. I wonder what that's about.* You might realize the other person is being a jerk! Or you might realize they're genuinely trying to help you out. Either way, it's an opportunity to name dissonance and free yourself from the following thinking traps.

Denial

Our minds are incredibly adept at helping us hide things from ourselves. Denial is when someone simply refuses to accept an inner tension. In the case of someone who's always tardy, they will flat-out deny it: "No, I'm not! I'm not tardy at all. I'm always on time." Or someone who has a drinking problem might deny how serious it is: "It's not a problem! I have it under control." Other types of denial are "I can stop at any time" or "It's not that big a deal."

The good news is that your mind and soul were designed to feel discomfort when you're in denial. The more you name the red flags of your own denial, the more you'll recognize it before it ensnares you.

Rationalization

Our minds are also amazing machines of rationalization. We love to create excuses for behaviors we don't feel great about. For example, let's say you make a large purchase that you can't afford. You rationalize it by thinking, *I deserve this!* Or you make a decision to skip a big family gathering, even though you care about your family. You might rationalize your behavior by telling yourself, *They don't really care if I'm there!*

We all rationalize from time to time. It's human. But when you rationalize a choice you make, you miss out on the opportunities for growth that surface only when you're honest with yourself. If you make a purchase you can't afford, it helps you grow to own it: *I made a mistake.* When you rationalize that others won't care if you are absent, you miss out on the opportunity for genuine connection: "I'm bummed I can't be with you. I love you. I miss you."

Perhaps you need to say no to a situation because it is painful—or even toxic—for you. Instead of rationalizing that choice (*I'm too busy!*), practice being honest with yourself: *It's hard for me to spend time with my family. I wish I had the kind of family I want to be with. The truth is I don't.* From that place you can then frame and brave a way to care for yourself.

Minimization

Minimization involves downplaying the importance or significance of an event, situation, or behavior as a way of avoiding your own internal discomfort. For example, you might minimize when someone hurts you. Maybe you pride yourself on being a low-maintenance friend. When your friend ignores you, it hurts. But you don't want to be a bother to them. So you cope by telling yourself, *Oh, it's nothing. I'm fine.* But, in fact, you're really hurt!

The problem is that if you make a habit of minimizing hurt, it doesn't go away. It festers. But when you name the hurt honestly, you can work to frame it correctly and determine the appropriate brave step. For example, you might decide to speak up to your friend: "I noticed you didn't reply to my last few texts. I wanted to check in to see what's up." It may be that you choose *not* to say anything. But you'll have made that decision from a place of self-respect and integrity. The more you trust yourself to speak up when something matters, the more you'll trust yourself when you decide that it's truly not a big deal.

All-or-Nothing Thinking

All-or-nothing thinking means you consider everything in binary terms. You tell yourself that things are only one thing or another, without considering the shades of gray, the nuances, the middle ground where so many things actually find their name. Here are some examples:

- *If I can't do it perfectly, I shouldn't do it at all.*
- *She disagreed with me, so she must not like me.*
- *If I make one mistake, the whole day is ruined.*
- *If I'm not the best, I'm the worst.*

When you think in these extreme terms, it makes it difficult to assess your own abilities and growth opportunities accurately. It also makes it hard to engage in healthy conversations with friends and romantic partners. When your spouse or friend gently tries to give you constructive feedback, you might feel shame, as if you are a complete failure. Instead of receiving that feedback and applying it, you might self-sabotage or get defensive: "I can't do anything right!"

But when you name a propensity for all-or-nothing thinking, you can start the work of creating holy reframes.

Negative Filters

Think of someone you know who has a hard time taking compliments. (Maybe it's you!) For example, you might hear a compliment but then find a way to reject it. Someone might say, "You did a great job organizing that program!" In response, you shrug it off, saying, "Oh, I didn't do anything. Everyone else made it happen!" When you have a negative filter, you filter out the positive and see yourself only through a negative lens.

You may not see yourself as someone who is worthy of praise. A compliment feels unnatural and jarring to you, so you find a way to brush it away, depriving yourself—and the other person—of an opportunity for connection. Just as the ability to give and receive constructive feedback is crucial to developing intimacy in relationships, so is the ability to give and receive genuine appreciation.

Sometimes we use negative filters to make sense of painful events. Instead of facing the pain of disappointment, you might tell yourself any of the following:

- *I'm just unlucky at love.*
- *Things will never get better.*
- *There's nothing I can do.*
- *I'm not good at anything.*

This was the trap Sheila was caught in when we first met. She had told herself she was unlucky at work and love. But such negative filtering doesn't help you find a way through legitimate struggles. If you believe you're unlucky at relationships, you may subconsciously create situations in which you sabotage your own efforts to make friends.[3]

On the other hand, when you name that it's hard for you to open up to the possibility of positive experiences, you can grow and change. You might practice naming this propensity to a friend: "Receiving that compliment feels so uncomfortable to me! I'm working on taking it in." In the very act of naming it, you've braved a bridge to deeper connection.

"Should" Statements

Your mind sometimes uses "should" statements to try to badger you into meeting an internalized set of expectations, the seeds of which are often planted by other people. You tell yourself the way you should or shouldn't think, feel, or act without necessarily reflecting on all the different truth-pieces.

- *I should be more successful by now.*
- *I shouldn't feel this angry, sad, or scared.*
- *I shouldn't need to ask for help.*
- *I should be more like _____.*

"Should" statements are a form of guilt-messaging yourself. When you notice a "should" statement repeatedly popping up in your mind, name it. Then name the expectation that statement represents. Is it one you want to keep? Or is it time to create a holy reframe?

When you recognize and name your thinking traps, you take a giant step toward freedom. It's no small feat to face yourself honestly, so please pause and affirm the good work you're doing. This is the work of becoming a Namer! You're starting by naming the contents of your own mind—one of the most powerful steps toward taking charge of your life.

Framing Thinking Traps

Now that you've named your thinking traps, it's time to frame them. Framing includes examining your thoughts, challenging unhelpful beliefs, and cultivating a more intentional and empowered perspective on your life. I cannot tell you how many times I ask clients these questions about the thoughts they entertain in their minds:

- Is that really true?
- Where did you pick up that belief about yourself?
- Is that a belief you want to keep?

Make it a regular practice to check in on your own thoughts each day. Identify a place in between where you'll examine your thoughts on a consistent basis using one of these strategies:

- Journal each morning to become aware of the thoughts in your mind.

- Take a walk each day to intentionally reflect on what you're thinking about.
- Turn off the radio when driving in the car and pay attention to what's on your mind.
- Keep a daily thought inventory on your phone. Note different thoughts that persist.
- Work with a therapist to help you better understand your thinking patterns.

Here are some examples of framing questions to ask yourself relative to the thinking traps you've identified:

- **Facts:** *When do I notice myself getting defensive? Who or what tends to provoke defensiveness in me? When do I notice myself rationalizing a behavior, minimizing, or slipping into all-or-nothing thinking? How often do I notice "should" statements in my mind?*
- **Roots:** *Why am I inclined to think this way? Where did I learn this way of thinking? Why do I want to change?*
- **Audit:** *How is this way of thinking helping me? How is it hurting me?*
- **Mental Messages:** *What fear comes up if I were to consider changing this way of thinking?*
- **Expansion:** *What would I say to a child or loved one who was thinking this way? What are some holy reframes I could create?*

Sometimes you need to outwit left-brain thinking traps by introducing them to your imagination. My favorite way to invoke my clients' imaginations is to ask questions that start with "What if":

- *What if* you could think about this in a different way?
- *What if* it's neither the worst-case scenario nor the best? What if it's somewhere in between?
- *What if* this compliment were true?
- *What if* you told the truth?

Finally, when you're framing a thinking trap, it can be helpful to ask yourself, *What am I afraid of?* The harder you work to rationalize, minimize, or defend yourself, the more likely it is that you're actually dealing with a tender emotion, an area of vulnerability, underneath. For example, I know I'm stuck in a thinking trap when my thoughts get all knotted up in a mental back-and-forth. It's as if I'm urgently trying to justify my position. When I notice that loop, I've learned to pause and take a deep breath: *What am I afraid of?* Nine times out of ten, I'm scared of being hurt or misunderstood. No amount of mental gymnastics is going to salve that root fear.

What *does* salve that fear is compassionate presence. *I get it. You're scared. That makes sense.* It's like unearthing a hidden belief that's been driving all that mental urgency—sometimes for years. That fear doesn't need your logic or mental gymnastics. It needs your care and compassion, your tender understanding.

Remember Sheila from the beginning of this chapter? On one hand, she had many talents and ambitions. She had a great education and many friends. But a tiny, albeit potent, fear had remained buried inside for years: *I'm not good enough. I don't have what it takes to make it in the real world.* Despite overwhelming evidence to the contrary, this fear was driving much of her decision-making—leading straight to self-sabotage. Not knowing any better, she'd tried to mask the shame she felt by attributing her challenges to bad luck. Sheila wanted more from her life. And she was capable of getting more. She began to align her thinking with the truth of her potential. Today she is one of the top nurses in her field, helping thousands of people get the care they need.

Thankfully, thinking traps don't work. The truth always finds its way out, if you're willing to do the work of naming, framing, and braving.

NAME, FRAME, AND BRAVE DISSONANCE

Name: What is an area of dissonance you notice inside? Which thinking trap (denial, rationalization, minimization, all-or-nothing thinking, negative filters, or "should" statements) are you most tempted to use to justify the dissonance?

Frame: What are the facts of the situation? Write a "two things can be true" holy reframe based on those facts.

Brave: What is a step you can take to honor the whole truth of the situation?

Braving a Change

When you work through thinking traps, you're engaging a scientifically backed process rooted in cognitive behavioral therapy. My adaptation of this process includes noticing what you're telling yourself (naming), reflecting on that (framing), and then actively working to change the way you respond to a situation (braving). You're shaping the contents of your mind and aligning your thoughts with reality. As you do this work, the next brave step will emerge. Suddenly you're moving. You're no longer stuck in your head.

The following chart illustrates how changing your thinking can lead to different types of braving steps.

Thinking Trap Chart

NAME THE TRAP	FRAME THE TRAP	BRAVE THE TRAP
It's not that big a deal.	This situation matters and I need to address it.	Tell someone you're noticing signs of relapse.
One little lie won't hurt anyone.	Each choice I make contributes to my habits and patterns.	Practice being honest: "I can't make it!"
I'm fine.	That comment hurt, and the impact was big. I need to address it with them.	Initiate a conversation with the other person.
I'm fine.	That comment hurt, and the impact was small. They don't often hurt me.	Consciously let it go.
I'm a failure, and I'll never get it right.	This project didn't go well. I've also done good work at other times.	Identify 2–3 areas you can improve on next time.
It was nothing—I didn't do much.	I feel grateful that someone noticed my hard work. I also feel uncomfortable.	Practice receiving a compliment: "Thank you!"
I shouldn't feel this way.	I do feel this way. This is a problem I need to address.	Ask a friend to help you process a challenge.

You might think of this work as equivalent to what the apostle Paul wrote: "Take every thought captive."[4] Often the biblical mandate to take every thought captive gets oversimplified. We apply it only to theological beliefs about God instead of applying it to the messages and thoughts we're believing about ourselves and the people in our lives. But the truth is that when I read the Bible with my therapist hat on, I see evidence of thinking traps in almost every story.

Consider King David. This is a man who loved God deeply, a man after God's own heart.[5] Yet somehow, over a period of time, a toxic thinking trap crept into his heart, soul, and mind. We see evidence of that toxic thinking when he acted on the impulse to assault Bathsheba and then attempted to cover up what he'd done by killing her husband.

We tend to read that story as if David suddenly did an atrocious thing out of nowhere. But that's not the way the human psyche works. More likely, that impulse was preceded by a widening incongruence, a dissonance that existed inside David for years. Over time he likely started rationalizing some of his behaviors. *I work so hard; I deserve this. It's not that bad. I'm a good person. Look at how much I'm doing for all these people!*

What might have started out as small missteps grew larger and larger, until one day he found himself committing grievous crimes. But here's the real tell of David's character: When he was confronted about his crimes, he admitted it. No defensiveness. He owned it, took responsibility, and bravely accepted a painful consequence.[6]

The true test of your character isn't that you never make mistakes; it's that you can own up to the mistakes you make and bravely change your ways.

This same idea is underscored in the New Testament, when you look at the missteps of two close friends of Jesus: Peter and Judas. Both men betrayed their friend, resulting in tremendous guilt and, no doubt, dissonance inside. When confronted with the disparity between his words and his actions, Peter admitted his betrayal. He also bravely received Jesus' forgiveness and affirmation of his worth, despite how ashamed he must have felt.

Judas did the opposite. We don't know exactly when Judas became aware of the tension inside him—the realization that he had betrayed a man he had once committed to honor. But we do know that he wasn't able to resolve the terrible feeling of that dissonance successfully, and he tragically ended his own life. We tend to demonize Judas for what he did to Jesus. But sometimes I wonder, *Was what Judas did that much worse than what Peter did? Or was the tragedy of Judas simply that he could not face the discomfort of his actions, name that discomfort, and take brave steps toward receiving Jesus' forgiveness and healing?*

Addressing your thinking traps is one of the most significant investments you can make in your mental and emotional health and in the quality of your life and relationships. When you take inventory of your thought life and bravely work to align your thoughts and actions with what's true, you become a powerful agent of change. You know when to speak up and when to hold back. You don't retaliate or make excuses when others criticize you. Instead, you show through the power of your actions that you are the one in command of you. You develop integrity, and you radiate authentic goodness to everyone around you.

SIX

I Shouldn't Feel Like Numbing My Emotions

"I don't know what's wrong with me!" Erika exclaimed. "Lately, several times a week, on my way home from work, I stop at a gas station, buy a big bag of potato chips, and down the entire bag in my car." As I asked her questions over the course of our first few sessions, it was clear she didn't fit the criteria for a full-fledged eating-disorder diagnosis. Her relationship with chips seemed to fall into a different category—compulsively reaching for them had become her secret way of numbing the stress of a new job.

Erika's secret numbing confession is only one of countless like it I've heard from clients and friends, and I've even noticed it in myself. Most people are struggling with some type of numbing behavior, and they're also beating themselves up for it. The truth is you probably weren't taught how to cope with painful emotions or stress in healthy ways. As a result, you may have learned to cope with pain by numbing your emotions or constantly distracting yourself.

Imagine a typical day. You're overwhelmed with too much to do. You've got a work deadline to meet and a couple of restless children who are home from school for the summer. Your house is a mess, and your refrigerator is empty. You're hosting friends for your weekly book club. You haven't eaten yet, and you can't remember the last time you combed your hair. As you anticipate the day ahead of you, your mind sounds a little like this: *I'm hungry. My house is a mess. Oh my gosh, I've got people coming over! I haven't prayed yet. I need to get to work. I really should exercise. I need to take a shower. What's wrong with me? I don't have time for any of this!*

And then the guilt messages enter in, adding pressure to what is already a pressure-filled situation: *I should learn to plan better. I always do this to myself! I really should work on setting better boundaries.*

The inner chaos of your mind starts to run roughshod over your best efforts.

And then the numbing kicks in.

You procrastinate and scroll social media for a few hours.

You stress-snack and empty an entire bag of cookies while cranking out your work.

You buy a brand-new set of dishes that you don't really need.

You pour yourself into organizing your garage instead of simply tidying up.

You compulsively counsel your friends while ignoring your own exhaustion.

You're unsure of how to tend to the chaos within your own mind, so you do something—anything—to distract yourself or remove all that pressure. And it becomes a downward spiral. The more you numb, the more you distract, the more your untended emotions ratchet up, the more you turn back to numbing.

All the while, your circumstances don't change. You might pull the day off. You might even meet the work deadline. But you feel terrible inside. Numbing keeps you from the chaos-shattering, light-breaking run-in with reality that empowers you to take charge of yourself and delight in your life.

The real problem or challenges you face aren't even getting named.

Numbing Emotions vs. Naming Emotions

Numbing is the opposite of naming. It's when you attempt to mute or suppress uncomfortable feelings. Instead of naming painful emotions, you try to make them go away—you work to keep them outside your conscious awareness. Numbing might work for a little while, but the problem is that those emotions don't go away. They linger untended in your body and soul, where they fester and create bigger problems over time.

Numbing can sneak up on you in several ways. It might start with minor distractions. For example, you might distract yourself from the stress of a hard day by scrolling social media, having a glass of wine, or binge-watching television. On any given day those actions might not become a problem. Maybe you get up the next morning and journal about what happened or

NUMBING IS THE OPPOSITE OF NAMING.

talk to a friend. You're dealing with what's hard. You're not forming a pattern. But if you consistently distract yourself day after day—and never face the reality of the underlying stress or painful emotions—you're likely to develop an unhealthy reliance on numbing behavior or possibly form an addiction.

Sometimes you learn to numb as a child. If no one taught you how to manage hard feelings, cope with pain, or self-soothe in healthy ways, you might have learned to numb yourself. In some cases, numbing was the only way to survive. I see this in my clients who turned to cutting themselves physically to soothe emotional pain. It can also show up in subtler ways. For example, when I was a child, if I felt lonely or anxious, I would sneak Dr Pepper out of our basement refrigerator and tiptoe back up to my bedroom, where I'd savor my delicious escape and then hide the empty cans in my bedroom closet. It wasn't until I was an adult that I made the connection between feeling stress or loneliness and emotional eating or drinking.

The problem of numbing is compounded by the fact that we live in an age when numbing and distractions are available to us as never before.[1] The options for numbing uncomfortable emotions—or distracting ourselves from them—in effortless and addictive ways are endless. Our hearts, minds, and bodies ache for care and attention, but counterfeit versions of comfort are everywhere. Instead of minding our minds, we drown out inner noise with outer distractions. Instead of slowing our bodies down, we amp them up with sugar, caffeine, or adrenaline. Instead of caring for our painful emotions, we get hooked on other people's drama. Instead of connecting with others, we mindlessly rush from appointment to appointment.

There is no shame in numbing. It's often a survival skill. It's also incredibly hard to avoid in our modern world. But it is a reality that we need to name and bravely face. Numbing creates bigger problems over time. It also keeps you from the real comfort and care your soul desperately needs.

Naming Numbing Behaviors

If you're feeling discontent or frustrated in your life but aren't exactly sure why, the first thing you might need to name is the very thing you've relied on to keep the pain away—you might need to name your numbing behavior.

Here are the most common examples of normal activities that can quickly turn into numbing behaviors:

- eating
- watching TV or movies
- browsing social media
- working
- helping others
- spending
- using substances (e.g., alcohol or pills)

Here's the thing: treating yourself to a favorite food or a snack, watching a great movie, or checking in with friends on social media can be great ways to care for yourself. Likewise, meeting needs, helping others, and immersing yourself in a work project can be wonderful things to do. Spending money as a way of improving your home or your mind or investing in projects can bring creativity and nourishment to your soul. When you do these activities mindfully, they can become a means to connect with others, spark imagination, or cope with stress.

Problems arise when otherwise healthy activities become numbing behaviors. You mindlessly eat, binge-watch, scroll, work, dive into someone else's problems, shop, or drink instead of tending to the needs of your heart. You're not naming what's hard and coping with it. You're numbing. For example, when I started having panic attacks in graduate school, I had never been more productive. I had also never been lonelier or more lost in my own unnamed pain. I love my work, and it is often a form of creative nourishment for me. But during this season I was using work to avoid facing what was hard in my life. In retrospect, I could see the clear correlation: the more pain I was in, the more I threw myself into my work. But at the time I simply thought I was being a productive, helpful citizen.

I see these same subtle numbing behaviors in my clients all the time. They avoid emotional pain by throwing themselves into taking care of their family or friends. Or they avoid the stress of their family life by throwing themselves into their work. Over the years I've heard countless namings of numbing behaviors. Here are some common examples:

- "I can't stop scrolling social media or streaming shows late at night. I'll stay up until three a.m., even though I'm exhausted."

- "Several times a week I find myself sneaking away to down a box of cookies or a big bag of chips. I feel terrible afterward, but I can't stop myself."
- "I compulsively buy things when I don't need them. I promise myself never to do it again, but it keeps happening."
- "I'm pouring myself a glass of wine (or two or three) almost every night. I know I need to stop, but I just keep doing it."

In each of these examples there are several clues that suggest the behavior is functioning as numbing: (1) The behavior is disrupting things you need, such as sleep, nutrition, connection with others, or financial stability. (2) The behavior is compulsive; you want to stop but you can't. (3) There's an element of secrecy; you don't want other people to find out what you're doing.

It's crucial to name numbing behaviors without shaming yourself. We often numb in secret, keeping the behaviors hidden from our conscious minds and from other people. Secrecy facilitates denial. It's also where shame festers. So when you start to name your numbing behaviors, be gentle with yourself. Name them in your journal. Name them to God. And when you do name them to someone else, ensure it's someone who will handle this naming with the care it deserves. Shame never helps.

The good news is that once you've named a numbing behavior, you're in a much better position to change it. Research suggests that getting honest about your numbing behaviors engages more of your thinking brain.[2] Once you've named it, you can then frame it and brave a way toward healthier coping tactics.

Framing Numbing Behaviors

The goal of framing, in this case, is to understand the dynamics of the numbing behavior and how it has helped you cope. As you explore the following questions, you might want to work with a therapist or a safe friend. When you reflect on your numbing behavior with someone who loves you and wants the best for you, it can help your progress exponentially.

Here are some questions to ask yourself when you're framing numbing behaviors:

- **Facts:** *When do I numb? Is it late at night? During the workday? On the weekend? How often does it happen?*
- **Roots:** *What triggers the numbing? Why do I want to change?*
- **Audit:** *What have I tried in the past to stop numbing? What worked? What didn't work?*
- **Mental Messages:** *What shaming messages do I tell myself about numbing? How can I reframe those messages in a compassionate way?*
- **Expansion:** *What are some proven ways of reducing this numbing behavior?*

You can also use the Looking Tool to reflect on the size and scope of the numbing behavior:

- **Looking Back:** *How long has this numbing behavior been a problem for me? Is it new, or is it something I've done for a long time?*

- **Looking at Today:** *What are other ways I can soothe or comfort myself?*
- **Looking Ahead:** *What would my life look like without this numbing behavior? What would change?*

Reflecting on these questions will help you get a bigger picture of your numbing behavior. They'll also help you gain insight into the emotions or events that are triggering it. For example, if you're mostly numbing late at night, you might be worried, stressed, or lonely. If you're tempted to numb after work or during the summer when your kids are home, it might be that you're tired or overwhelmed. You can then begin to identify brave steps to change your numbing behavior.

Braving a Change

The goal of braving is to reduce the numbing behavior and replace it with a more beneficial option. There are several ways to do this. You might fight for a healthier relationship with a specific numbing behavior or you might suffer it wisely for a clear reason. You might leave a numbing behavior behind entirely. No matter which choice you make, you'll need to expand your range of healthy ways to care for yourself.

When you fight for a behavior, you work to preserve the good that you enjoy in moderation. For example, I have a lifelong love affair with pizza. At times that relationship has grown unhealthy; I've turned to pizza—lots of pizza—in secrecy to get comfort when I felt anxious or lonely. The problem is that while pizza is great, it's not actually the friend I need in moments of pain or loneliness. When an impulse to reach for pizza surfaces, I remind myself that, for me, it is a comfort best enjoyed with other people. That reframe helps me not to shame myself in the moment, which in turn helps me make a wiser choice. I then choose one of the alternatives I've identified that provide true comfort—I take a walk down my favorite trail, listen to music that matches my mood, or Vox with a friend.

You can apply this same moderation technique to other behaviors such as scrolling social media or spending. For example, pick one day a week to scroll or post on social media. Enjoy scrolling on that one day, then delete your social media apps for the rest of the week. Or you might fight for the opportunity to enjoy making a fun purchase. Schedule a shopping date with yourself and write it on your calendar. Then remove your credit card from online shopping sites, creating friction to prevent acting on an impulse.[3] If you're tempted to break out the credit card, remind yourself *I really want to give myself this gift next month!* Choose an alternative way to soothe yourself in that moment instead.

You may determine, after framing, that you're going to suffer certain numbing behaviors wisely. I've worked with clients who rely on television to help them deal with loneliness at night. It's interfering with their sleep, but it's also providing much-needed distraction. When that's the case, we talk about how to minimize the intrusion. For example, tuning in to an audiobook can be less disruptive to your sleep than staring at the blue light of a screen. Setting a timer on your device ensures that it switches off after a certain amount of time.

In another case, I worked with a client who was processing the trauma of childhood abuse for the first time. During the height of this emotional season, she started beating herself up that she couldn't give up smoking just as she was about to confront her parents. I gently helped her to frame the reality of all she was asking of herself at this time. Did she want to give up smoking? Yes. Was now the best time? No. She decided to talk to a psychiatrist about alternative ways of managing anxiety before she weaned herself off cigarettes.

If you have multiple numbing habits, you might focus on removing one, while choosing to suffer another one wisely for a time—you prioritize leaving behind the one that is causing the most harm. The most important thing is to be mindful of your decisions in a non-shaming way. Remember, braving means taking one small step at a time.

Finally, you might decide that you need to leave your numbing behavior behind altogether. In this case you're going to brave a detox. A detox is a process of removing something toxic from your body, allowing yourself the opportunity to learn to function without that toxin. You need a period of time—a place in between—to allow yourself to adjust to living without that numbing device. And you also need to choose other, healthier ways to cope.

As you reduce your dependence on a numbing behavior, you'll likely notice new feelings that surface, vulnerable feelings that may be uncomfortable or unpleasant. Don't be alarmed. Those vulnerable feelings present you with a new opportunity to name, frame, and brave a healthier way to care for yourself.

Name, Frame, and Brave a Detox

Sometimes you notice the negative side effects of numbing before you become aware of the numbing behavior itself. That was the case for me.

One of my favorite naming tools is the daily practice of journaling. In many ways I've learned to see my daily naming as a form of confession. It also becomes a form of self-accountability—when you are relentlessly honest about naming what's hard each day, you start to notice patterns. A few years ago, I noticed myself naming thoughts like these almost every single day: *I'm frustrated with myself. I'm resentful and angry. I feel cynical about other people.*

I didn't normally feel this resentful or cynical. It wasn't in my character, so to speak. I liked my life—I loved my family, my friends, my work. It didn't make sense that I was feeling so much negativity inside me. I decided I needed to take myself to the Crossroads and figure out what this was all about. I named my problem "Negativity" and set out to frame it.

As I moved about my day—grocery shopping, walking the dogs, or running errands—I began to reflect on this newfound negativity with prayerful intentionality.

What has changed in my life to evoke this negativity? I thought, as I talked to God, running through the framing questions I'd learned to ask myself. *When do I feel the negative emotions? How long have they been here?*

As I thought about the past few months and paid closer attention to my daily activities, the truth suddenly smacked me in the face. Each of those negative emotions could be traced to the simple but profound action of opening my Instagram app. Every time I opened my feed, which was way more often than I liked to admit, I would notice myself getting sucked in by something someone else had posted. And then, almost subconsciously, a wash of negativity would flood over me.

Frustration.

Resentment.

Cynicism.

I could not believe I had missed this clear, albeit insidious, link between a simple act of scrolling and my mood.

What complicated the problem for me was that social media was part of my job. It was the primary way in which I connected with people who followed my work and listened to my podcast. I didn't want to disappoint people I truly cared about, but the negativity was beginning to steal the joy I felt in my work. So I decided that the cost of taking a break from social media was worth the risk. It was time to brave a six-week social media detox and discern a healthier way of connecting with other people.

Initially, it felt great to delete Instagram off my phone, as if a chain had been removed from my soul. The first few days of the detox, I could not believe how quiet my mind felt. All I noticed was the sheer absence of noise—the blissful departure of the flashing, dancing circus of my feed. I also began to notice how much data I had absorbed about people I didn't even know. I knew all about Tom and Gisele's divorce. I knew the names of Jen Hatmaker's children, even though I've never met her or them. Why in the world was my mind tracking this information?

My incessant app checking had also created some other

compulsive habits. I had reverted down an old path of being ever available through text messages. I was compulsively responding to requests from other people instead of taking my time to think through whether, when, or how to respond.

As I detoxed, I became more aware of a regular impulse to check my phone, even though Instagram was now gone. I observed my hand starting to reach for my phone, only to freeze in midair as I realized there was nothing there for it to check. That split-second noticing was enough to remind me to take a deep breath and create a place in between where I could evaluate my next move. I began to bask in the new spaciousness that my social media detox had opened up to me.

Then came the withdrawal. Fear showed up a few days after the calm. I started to worry about the ramifications of being off social media. *Will I disappoint the people who follow me? How will I connect with other people I don't see regularly? What if people forget about me?*

So I began to name and frame the fear: *I see you there, fear. I understand. It's scary to make a change.* I didn't gaslight myself or try to logic it away; I engaged it from a loving place. I then began to gently remind myself that two things can be true. *You might disappoint some people,* and *you need to do this for your own health. You might disappoint some people,* and *you might inspire others who also struggle with social media.*

Fear started to dissipate. I began to build more trust with myself.

Over time, as I attuned to myself in this new fashion, my joy returned in countless ways. I was more aware of my own needs and could meet them. I was more present to my family and the people in my real life. My creativity and imagination started showing up again.

I hadn't realized they'd been gone, those old friends who, in moments of quiet or boredom, delighted me with whimsical impulses to dance, take an adventure, or be silly. I found my way back to play and rest and a peaceful mind.

As I named the negativity and braved a detox, I began to see how my relationship with social media would need to change. I wasn't going to leave it behind altogether. But I was going to have to figure out how to suffer it wisely. I would need to brave a new way to use it while holding on to all I'd recently discovered.

Below the Surface of Numbing Behaviors

There are typically two layers to work through when you're naming, framing, and braving numbing behaviors. The first layer is the numbing activity itself. It's usually the more obvious, surface-level issue, such as working too much, scrolling too much, throwing yourself into the pain of others (codependency), or emotional eating. The second layer, however, is equally crucial to address. It's the painful emotions that lead to the numbing.

Like thinking traps, numbing is almost always self-protective. There's a reason you do it—typically to prevent the experience of painful or vulnerable feelings.[4] Here are seven common emotions that may surface as you work to eliminate your numbing behaviors:

- shame
- fear
- self-doubt

- guilt
- a sense of being unseen, unappreciated, or overlooked
- loneliness
- sadness

And, as a bonus, sometimes anger will surface. Women especially often numb themselves as a way to avoid feeling the uncomfortable emotion of anger.[5]

When you notice any of these feelings, you might be tempted to head right back to that numbing behavior. A bag of chips or an online shopping spree can certainly drown out a painful emotion— for a moment. But remember the words of wise King Solomon: there is "a time to weep and a time to laugh, a time to mourn and a time to dance."[6] There's a time to feel your sadness, your loneliness, and even your anger. As Stanford psychiatrist Anna Lembke wrote in her insightful book *Dopamine Nation*, "With intermittent exposure to pain . . . we become less vulnerable to pain and more able to feel pleasure over time."[7] In other words, to keep pain from becoming too big, you need to tend to the right amount of pain in healthy ways.

THERE'S A TIME TO FEEL YOUR SADNESS, YOUR LONELINESS, AND EVEN YOUR ANGER.

How do you tend to your pain? Start by naming it.

I'm scared.

I'm anxious.

I'm lonely.

I'm exhausted.

Remember, naming in and of itself brings some relief. You're finally at the root. You've painstakingly and lovingly gained access to a sacred place of need. You can now do the work of identifying the good things your mind, heart, and body crave. Take a deep breath or move your location and ask yourself the following framing questions:

What do *I need in this moment?*

What would *soothe my fear, my anxiety, my loneliness?*

What would *bring my exhausted body relief?*

Here's the good news: you can learn to replace numbing behaviors with the care you actually need.

BRAVING CARE

Choose several activities from each of the following categories. Practice caring for yourself in these ways when you notice an urge to numb.

- **Relational Care:** Talking with a safe friend, attending a support group, spending time with family, playing with children, or enjoying animals can provide comfort, empathy, or understanding.
- **Sensory Care:** Listening to music, lighting a candle, wrapping up in a soft blanket, or immersing yourself in a beautiful setting can soothe your senses and evoke feelings of calm, warmth, and contentment.
- **Recreational Care:** Gardening, cooking, painting,

playing sports, or watching a movie can help you process negative emotions and inspire creativity.

- **Physical Care:** Exercising, taking a walk, hydrating, practicing deep breathing, or stretching can help you feel rested, nourished, and rejuvenated.
- **Spiritual Care:** Praying, meditating, reading Scripture, or singing songs of praise can bring solace, perspective, and encouragement.

The Goodness Your Soul Craves

Naming, framing, and braving numbing behaviors isn't about becoming a machine of rigid self-denial, nor is it the drudgery of willpower. It's the opposite! It's attuning to the intricacies of your mind, heart, and body and learning what brings you comfort, relief, peace, or delight. It's bravely refusing the counterfeit comforts and deadening distractions that beckon you from every direction. It's turning toward the goodness your soul craves, the goodness all around you.

We need play. We need rest. We need comfort. We need to escape through the power of our imaginations. These are all good things. The Enemy of our souls has excelled at distorting otherwise good gifts and turning them into shackles. When we're constantly checking our phones—our feeds, the news, our texts—or distracting ourselves in countless other ways, we're not creating those quiet places in between where real rest and deep nourishment occur.

Numbing your emotions keeps you from the wild, purposeful, sometimes scary, deeply important life God created you to live out. On the other hand, naming your emotions empowers you to care for yourself and shape your reality as you align with God's mission of turning chaos into harmony and infusing life with goodness.

When you name, you come alive to yourself and to God and to the wonder all around you. You feel that wild surge of aliveness as you savor the feeling of fresh soil under your feet or lose yourself in the starry sky as night descends. You honor the tears that well up in your eyes as a tender moment overtakes you. You delight in the laughter that bursts forth as you rehash a child's antics. You marvel at the flash of insight or the epiphany that comes when the dots of a problem you've been wrestling with suddenly connect. You cherish the surprised yet grateful feeling in your heart as you contemplate a loved one's actions. You are transformed by the almost imperceptible voice of God's Spirit whispering, *Your life is precious.*

SEVEN

I Shouldn't Feel Ashamed of My Body

So many of us don't know how to live in our bodies. We've never been taught what that means. We know we "should" care for our bodies, but so often those guilt messages become the only messages we tell ourselves.

I should eat healthier.

I should exercise.

I should do this.

I shouldn't do that.

I shouldn't feel this way about my body.

Talk about dissonance! We want to feel healthy in our bodies, but so often we ignore their cries for help or the warning signals they send. We analyze, criticize, or guilt-message ourselves about our bodies. We might even abuse or neglect them, only to give them a quick fix when their poor, tired selves beg for our attention. We don't treat our bodies very well. We don't understand our bodies very well.

This has certainly been my experience, and it's the experience of many of my clients. Yet our bodies need us, and we need our bodies. For most of my life my body was an afterthought. Until its cries for attention finally started to reach me. If you read my book *The Best of You*, you know that I had a stroke in the fall of 2020. I wish I could say that day changed everything. But it didn't. While I attended numerous doctor's appointments and underwent a lot of medical testing, none of this really changed how I related to my body.

In the aftermath of that trauma, I prayed, I journaled, I tended to my emotions. All those things were helpful. But it wasn't until I braved my detox from social media that I realized the depth of my own disembodiment. As I paused in the in-between places—now freed from numbing and distractions—I began to notice the cries of a body begging for my attention.

At the Crossroads with Our Bodies

Your body is so much more than a frame for your outward appearance. It weaves together all the different pieces of your soul through a complex system of neurons and cells and the nervous system, with your brain at its epicenter. It encases your soul with skin and hair. It has eyes to see, ears to hear, and a mouth to express and interact with the world around you. Your body serves as your visible presence in the world—it keeps you from being invisible.

Your body is also intimately involved in all your decisions. Your nervous system not only orchestrates your physical movements but also helps you process feelings of fear, joy, pain, and stress. It detects threats and mobilizes you to take action. It carries the burdens of past trauma, often silently, on your behalf.

The problem is that we don't know what to do with this body that leaves us feeling so vulnerable: vulnerable to painful emotions, to sickness, and to scrutiny. Vulnerable to a world that can feel dangerous. So often we secretly despise our bodies for not shielding us from pain, shame, and judgment from others. It's hard to inhabit a body.

Instead of fully inhabiting our bodies—caring for them and allowing them to care for us—we attempt to sideline them. We prioritize our minds, emotions, or spiritual lives, treating our bodies like an inconvenient chore. If you relate to what I'm saying, please know there's no shame in any of this. In many ways we've learned to disparage our bodies as a form of survival. But in order to heal, it's important to recognize some of the names we've silently given our bodies:

- broken
- embarrassing
- shameful
- disgusting
- cumbersome
- ugly
- weak
- wrinkled
- scrawny

- fat
- old
- scarred

Even when we don't consciously use names like these, we tend to disregard the cues that our bodies are desperately trying to send us.

Why can't I just get it together? we say to ourselves, instead of noticing tension or a sudden onset of exhaustion as an opportunity to name something that feels hard—and taking the opportunity to gently care for ourselves.

Stop being so anxious! we yell at ourselves, instead of reflecting, *I wonder what my body is trying to tell me.*

If, as I have, you've named or guilt-messaged your body in any of these ways, I promise you that we can change. Together, we can build a healthier framework through which to view our bodies.

Framing Your Body in a New Way

It makes sense that we don't know how to honor our bodies. Historically, both faith traditions and psychology approaches have been slow to recognize and honor our bodies as sacred, and they have been slow to acknowledge that our bodies are integral not only to our physical health but to our emotional, mental, and spiritual health.[1] We now know that our mind and emotions are intimately connected and interrelated with our bodies.[2]

Culturally, our bodies have been stigmatized and simplified in every single way—including ideas about beauty, respect, value, and worth. We are slowly learning to see our bodies as worthy of honor in all the nuances of each body's design. But this realization is in its infancy when contrasted with centuries of misguided perceptions. In short, we've inherited a long and complicated history of toxic distortions, half-truths, and guilt-driven messages about the body.

At best, you may have been taught the basics of nutrition, sleep, and exercise. At worst, you may have been taught—whether explicitly or through other people's actions—that your body is shameful, bad, or unworthy of love. You may have been taught that your body should look a certain way. You may have been taught that it's your fault if other people abused or objectified your body.

If you received any of these messages about your body, I'm so sorry. These messages are wrong, and you deserve better. The Enemy of your soul knows how valuable your body is and how vulnerable it is. There's a reason why he's unleashed his strongest attacks on it. But with God's help you can create a powerful new frame.

As you frame a new way of viewing your body, consider the following questions:

- **Facts:** *What was I taught about my body? Where did I learn those messages?*
- **Roots:** *Why does the way I view my body matter?*
- **Audit:** *When have I felt connected to my body in a healthy way? When have I felt shame or frustration with my body?*
- **Mental Messages:** *What messages do I tell myself about my body? How do I think God sees my body?*
- **Expansion:** *What are other perspectives about my body I'd like to learn?*

You can also use the Looking Tool to capture a bigger picture of how you've related to your body:

- **Looking Back:** *How did I feel about my body as a child? As a teen?*
- **Looking at Today:** *How do I feel about my body now?*
- **Looking Ahead:** *How would I like to feel toward my body five years from now? Ten years from now? Twenty years from now? What would progress look like?*

As you reflect on how you've related to your body in the past and how you'd like to honor your body in the future, it's crucial to create and practice holy reframes. For example, what if you could begin to consider new names for your body, like these?

Instead of exhausted: *My body needs care.*

Instead of weak: *My body is intricate and nuanced.*

Instead of broken: *My body is healing.*

Instead of ugly: *My body is beautifully made.*

Instead of old: *My body is wise.*

Instead of scarred: *My body is resilient.*

Instead of shameful: *My body is a masterpiece.*[3]

Intentionally reframing the way you view your body is a brave step in and of itself. As you spend time in your place in between each day, notice the messages you tell yourself about your body. When you notice shaming self-talk, gently redirect your thoughts to your holy reframe. Over time you'll begin to experience your body as a sacred vessel, the ship you get to lovingly steer into the wide-open waters of your life.[4]

Braving Embodiment

Sometimes when you enter the Crossroads, you realize you need to make a major change in direction. As you start to move in this new direction, you realize this isn't going to be a minor tweak. You'll need to make a giant, whole-body shift.

When I think of a whole-body shift, I think of a large cruise ship out on the ocean that has drifted off course. Ever so slowly and ever so steadily, the captain of the ship must shift the entire vessel so that it moves in a different direction. The shift requires several complex and coordinated actions, such as adjusting the rudder and monitoring navigation systems. It's not a quick change. Similarly, shifting how you guide your body requires a coordinated effort of adjusting old thinking traps and acquiring new habits. It's not just practicing more self-care. It's not just "accepting your body," though each of those things is important. The new course you have to brave is deeper than that. The goal is to fully inhabit your body. You achieve that goal by attuning to the big and small signals it sends you each day.

When you attune to someone else, you become aware of and responsive to their emotional states and needs. Often you are attuning to nonverbal cues. A mother attunes to her baby when she searches for clues for why the baby might be crying. You attune to a loved one when you seek to understand a downcast facial expression or slumped posture. Likewise, you attune to your body when you notice and respond to the various cues it is sending, such as fatigue, tension, hunger, a pit in your stomach, or an increased heart rate. Each of these cues represents more than a physical state—it's also a clue to your emotional state and your environment. In other words, as you attune to your body, you attune to your whole being.

AS YOU ATTUNE TO YOUR BODY, YOU ATTUNE TO YOUR WHOLE BEING.

This is what I realized as I detoxed from social media and began to notice how often I had ignored the signals my body was sending me—I needed to brave a completely new way of attuning to my body.

As I became more aware in the quiet of the detox, my mind calm and attentive, I noticed that my body was constantly giving me nudges to let me know what it needed. Every time I was tempted to reach for food or my phone, I'd pause and engage a tiny place in between. *What is my body trying to tell me?*

Do I need a snack?

Pause.

Water?

Pause.

Am I tired?

Pause.

What does my body need?

Each pause helped me to retrain my brain to attune to the signals my body was sending me. Instead of bribing myself with a pseudo solution or dopamine hit, I began to ask framing questions. *Am I tense? Hunched over? How long have I been sitting here?* Inevitably, I'd notice that I'd been sitting for hours at my desk, not moving, hardly aware of my slumping shoulders or aching back. Without even realizing it, I'd trained myself to pick up my phone or grab a snack whenever my brain registered a cue that my body was tired or in need of a break.

But now I could harness that very action that had been causing so much negativity—reaching for my phone—to help me attune to the actual needs of my body. Each tiny pause led to a tiny adjustment that eventually led to complete overhaul of how I related to my body, my work, and my entire day.

Instead of stress-snacking and scrolling, I developed a whole new repertoire of activities: Move around the house. Untense. Slowly roll my neck and shoulders. Stretch my back. Take a walk outside. Drink water. Dance it out to my favorite song.

And so commenced one of the subtlest, yet one of the most profound, experiences of healing I've had. I began to attune to my body. I began to work with my body instead of against her. I began to care, genuinely, for my own body. And in return, she started caring for me.

The truth is that this change didn't happen overnight. Early on I bumped up against internal resistance. *This doesn't feel very good! Isn't it easier to just numb? Why wouldn't I stay buried in my work, in other people's problems, or in seemingly harmless distractions?*

And so I named and framed those feelings too. *I get it. Change is hard. It's new. Two things can be true: You're letting some things go. You're also doing what you've so long known you needed to do.*

And one brave step at a time, I began to experience embodiment.

The subtle work of braving embodiment can feel seismic at first. It's an awakening. Slowly, you start to realize that your body is the very best sort of friend. A friend who gently speaks up when you're overextending yourself. A friend who lets you know when you need a rest. A friend who lights up with joy when you shower it with good, nourishing activities. A friend who loves you back.

THE GOAL ISN'T TO CONTROL YOUR BODY, THE GOAL IS TO ATTUNE TO YOUR BODY'S NEEDS.

The goal isn't to control your body; the goal is to attune to your body's needs. Your body naturally moves from states of stress to states of need to states of strength. That's what it's supposed to do! In her beautiful book *Strong Like Water*, trauma therapist Aundi Kolber described this movement as a "flow of strength."[5] As you attune to your body's needs, you form a reciprocal relationship with it. You recognize when your body is in need, and your body in turn helps you to regulate emotions, gain clarity of thought, and step up when you need to protect yourself. You start to recognize some of the following connections.

Movement really does help my mood.

Taking deep breaths slows my anxious mind.

I feel calmer when I release the tension in my neck.

As you participate in this flow of strength, you experience your body as integral to your mental, emotional, and spiritual health. You learn to value your body as if it is indeed God's masterpiece.

BRAVING A CALM NERVOUS SYSTEM

Through developing an awareness of the signals your body is sending, you can learn to calm your nervous system.[6] Here are a few research-backed exercises to add to your range of braving steps.

- **Deep breathing:** Take a deep breath all the way into your belly. A common method is the 4-7-8 technique— inhale for four seconds, hold your breath for seven seconds, and exhale for eight seconds. Then repeat the cycle a few times.[7]
- **Guided imagery:** Imagine a safe place in your mind. You might imagine a beach, with the sound of waves crashing and the feel of sun on your skin. You might imagine yourself standing on a mountain peak, feeling the cool breeze, or in a safe, protective space, like a cozy cabin where you feel entirely secure and at ease.[8]
- **Grounding exercises:** Connect to your five senses. You might run cold water over your hands or slowly tense and untense different muscle groups in your body. You might slowly and consciously become aware of what you can see, hear, smell, touch, and taste from where you're sitting or standing.[9]
- **Nature bathing:** Get outside without your phone. Stroll through a city park, botanical gardens, or simply walk down a tree-lined street. If possible, visit a body of water or go to the mountains. Research shows that spending at least twenty minutes outdoors three days a week without technology improves your overall well-being.[10]

God Came in a Body

This idea that the body matters is as ancient as the days. It is not a new idea. Despite several ancient heresies that denied the goodness of the body,[11] orthodox Christian theology maintains that the body is an integral part of the human person, a part of the goodness of God's creation. This view of the body is rooted in the belief that God created human beings in his image and likeness.[12] God called his creation good before sin entered in, and that creation includes the body.

We see the dignity of the body illustrated in numerous ways throughout Scripture. In John 14, when Jesus promised the coming of the Holy Spirit, he said that it would dwell within our bodies. Paul expanded on this point when he said, "The physical part of you is not some piece of property belonging to the spiritual part of you. God owns the whole works. So let people see God in and through your body."[13] Your body is the dwelling place for the living God. It's a place of honor, a place that is sacred, a place to tend with care and wonder, as you might care for any sacred dwelling.

And, finally, we see the dignity in the body in the fact that Jesus came in a body.[14]

Jesus lived in a body.

Jesus died in a body.

Jesus was resurrected in a body.

Too often we gloss over the reality of what that statement means: Jesus was resurrected *in a body*. His resurrected body bore the wounds of his life as a human on earth.[15] It was the same body, even though it looked a little different. At the ascension, when Jesus returned to heaven, his body went with him.[16] The physical ascension of Jesus suggests that our bodies will still be with us on the other side of this life.

Your body is not an inconvenience. It's not something to put up with until you become a disembodied soul in heaven. Your body matters. It matters now, and it matters for all eternity.

Loving Your Body as a Spiritual Practice

It's as important to your overall well-being to tune in to your body each day as it is to tune in to your mind, your heart, and your spirit. All these brave actions honor God. To love God means to love the body God gave you. To love your body is a part of what it means to honor God.

Each morning when you pray or journal, you might practice naming, framing, and braving a new message, a love note to your body: *My body is precious. My body helps me make wise decisions. My body needs me just as much as other people need me. My body is valued by God.*

You might also welcome your body into expressions of emotion and prayer. Shonda Rhimes was onto something profound when she had her characters "dance it out" on *Grey's Anatomy*. Dancing it out—whether by yourself when no one's watching or with a group of loves ones—can be a profound way to release tears, evoke joy, and even metabolize anger.

Is this what it meant that "David danced before the LORD with all his might"?[17] That he worked out all the mixed-up, complicated emotions of his life and expressed them through his body before God? That he found a way to communicate with God with his whole body?

What if learning to live in your body and, more importantly, learning to honor your body go hand in hand with loving God? What if this act of honoring your body *is* a spiritual practice?

EIGHT

I Shouldn't Feel Less Than Other People

My client Erin was an expert at observing the lives of others. When I asked her simple questions about what she wanted from her life, she almost immediately brought up someone else: "I see my friends posting photos of their families all the time. One of them is always traveling. Another one got divorced but already found a new boyfriend—she's having so much fun! My mom tells me I should get off social media and learn to be content. But I just feel like my life is so boring in comparison to theirs."

While I listened to Erin, I found myself in a mental game of pinball, trying to track the ball that pinged between the different people she'd bounce off as she attempted to answer a question about her own life. I was getting lost in all the people she was tracking, and I could only imagine how it must have felt for her inside.

So I tried a different tactic. I asked her about herself as if she were another person.

"And what about Erin?" I asked. "What does *she* want?"

Erin stopped for a moment. Her eyes grew soft as she contemplated that question. "I'm not sure," she finally responded. "I guess I thought I was supposed to want what everybody else has."

As time went on, it became clear that Erin was disconnected from her own sense of self. She couldn't gauge her own desires, interests, or callings. She wasn't even sure that it would be possible for her to do that. Instead, she constantly looked to other people to try to ascertain the life she thought she should have. She was stuck in a rut of comparison and had no idea how to name, frame, and brave her way into a life she actually wanted.

The Problem with Comparison

If you've found yourself caught in the rut of comparison, you're not alone. Research suggests that our propensity to compare ourselves to others has increased dramatically with the introduction of the internet and social media. But the truth is that comparison has been around well before social media provided constant access to it. Social psychologist Leon Festinger began to study what he called "social comparison theory" as early as 1954, noting its ambivalent impact on our lives.[1] It's natural to gauge your own success by comparing your life to the lives of others. Most people do it. Although comparison can sometimes be healthy and even inspire or motivate you to make positive changes, it can also have negative effects, such as lowering self-esteem, increasing depression, and promoting a self-sabotaging mentality.[2]

Current research indicates that the addition of social media to our daily lives has primarily increased the negative effects of social comparison.[3] Instead of focusing on naming, framing, and braving the life *you* want to live and the values *you* want to adopt, you become distracted, confused, and discouraged as you constantly try to measure up to what you perceive to be happening in the lives of other people.

It's one thing to be influenced positively by someone else's successes, to push yourself to improve an aspect of your life; it's another thing to constantly criticize or guilt-message yourself in comparison to others to the point that you start to dislike yourself or them. The difference between constructive comparison and unhealthy comparison is in the fruit it bears. Constructive comparison is empowering—it motivates you to become your best self. Unhealthy comparison produces negative results, such as helplessness, self-defeat, and resentment.

Name, Frame, and Brave Comparison

There are a number of root causes of unhealthy comparison, each one requiring a different remedy. To break free from the negative impact of comparison, first, name what lies at the root. You can then frame and brave a way out of comparing yourself to others and into claiming the life God has given *you* to live. Here are a few of the most common causes of comparison and several ways to frame and brave them.

A Comparing Inner Critic

Often, a ferocious inner critic drives us to compare ourselves to others. If you ever notice thoughts like these, self-criticism may be to blame.

She's better than me.

I should be able to parent, lead, or _____ perfectly, like they are!

I'll never be as fun, smart, successful, or _____ as she is.

This inner critic is well intentioned, believe it or not. But its strategies are incredibly unhelpful. It tries to motivate you by holding up other people as the ideal. The problem is the ideal doesn't really exist. No one's doing life as well as you might think they are. It's also an ever-moving target. The minute you reach one ideal, another one will appear that's even loftier. Because you'll never live up to the ideal, you wind up running on a never-ending treadmill exhausted, resentful, and discontented. You remain at odds with yourself and frustrated by the success of other people. And you never really experience the satisfaction and deep-down joy in your own accomplishments that God intends for you to experience.

Sometimes this inner critic turns outward, and you become critical or judgmental of others in order to build yourself up.

Their kids misbehave way more than mine do.

I would never do that! At least I don't lose my temper like he does!

Thank goodness I'm funnier, smarter, more successful, or _____ than they are.

Your inner critic takes a secret joy in pointing out someone else's failures as a way of making you feel better. But you're still comparing yourself to others. It's a pseudo solution, and it doesn't lead to genuine confidence or satisfaction. No matter whether your critic is inner or outer, you're looking to others to set your standard rather than focusing on the work of aligning your goals, gifts, and values to the God who made you, the one who truly sets your standard.

Naming a comparing inner critic can bring relief in itself. When you name something, you differentiate from it—you get healthy distance from it, which allows you to take command. When you notice thoughts like *She's better than me* or *At least I'm not as bad as they are*, you don't have to allow those thoughts to drive you. Instead, name the thoughts for what they are: *Oh, that's my inner critic!* or *Gosh, I keep criticizing myself.* Or *I keep criticizing that other person.* Then notice and name the event that precipitated the internal comparison.

Once you've named your inner critic, you can frame its role in your life. Use your places in between, such as a walk, drive, or morning journaling session, to reflect on this aspect of yourself and ask yourself these questions:

- **Facts:** *What situations magnify my inner critic? What situations allow me to get some space from it?*
- **Roots:** *How long has my inner critic been with me? What is an early memory of criticism?*
- **Audit:** *Is criticizing myself or others working as a strategy to motivate me?*
- **Mental Messages:** *What do I fear would happen if I stopped criticizing myself?*
- **Expansion:** *How do trusted people in my life view my inner critic? What is a more effective way to motivate myself?*

Pay attention to see if your inner critic has a spiritual component. Sometimes it can feel as if your inner critic is masquerading as the voice of God: *You're not worthy!* or *You're not doing as much as other people!* Remember: God isn't cruel or judgmental. Nor does he compare one of his children to another. God comes alongside you with patience and kindness, in gentle, truth-filled ways.[4]

Inner critics also keep you stuck in thinking traps, such as all-or-nothing thought patterns or "should" statements. *I'm a failure if I don't have her success. I should be more like other people. I'll never be as good as other people.* Sometimes you even get stuck in thinking traps about your loved ones. *My kids will never be as good as theirs.* When you find this happening, make a list of those key phrases. Next to each one write a holy reframe—one steeped in deep compassion. Here are a few examples:

- *I'm a failure if I don't have her success* **becomes** *I want to be my best self.*
- *I'll never be as good as other people* **becomes** *No one can take my place.*
- *My kids will never be as good as theirs* **becomes** *No one can take their place.*
- *I should be more _____* **becomes** *I like that I'm _____.*

Write your reframe in your phone or on a sticky note that you attach to your mirror. When you notice yourself preoccupied by any of these self-critical thoughts, take a deep breath and shift your mental focus to the reframe. Ask God to meet you in that place in between where your self-critical thoughts have been and this new neural pathway you're working to blaze.

The work of moving toward self-compassion is a brave step. It actually changes the physiology of your body.[5] Criticism stimulates the body's stress response, which includes the release of adrenaline. Your pulse quickens and cortisol is released, and you become more tense. When you practice self-compassion, however, you activate the "rest and digest" part of your nervous system, helping your body to move toward relaxation, rest, and recovery. You lower your heart rate and blood pressure, which reduces stress hormones. You untense your body. When your nervous system is calm, your brain tends to function more effectively, increasing your capacity for perspective and creativity.

Remember: brave actions flow from clear minds. When you name your inner critic, you begin to tame it. You can create a plan to mitigate the damaging effects of comparison before it gets the better of you. You might leave certain situations or greatly reduce your exposure to them. For example, if certain feeds on social media provoke your comparing inner critic, mute them. If you're part of a group or club that constantly activates your comparing inner critic, consider taking a break from it.

In other cases you'll need to fight for change. For example, if you're struggling financially while your best friend constantly talks about her lavish expenditures, you might need to speak up on behalf of what you need: "Money brings up complicated emotions for me. I'm working on it. But in the meantime, could we talk about something else?" Or if your mom always brings up how wonderful everyone else's kids are—while never praising your kids—you might need to confront her behavior or advocate for yourself: "Mom, I am really hard on myself. When you talk about other people's kids, it stirs up negative feelings of comparison inside me. Could you tell me something that you're proud of in me or the kids?"

Finally, you'll need to suffer comparison wisely in some situations. You can't fight for change, and you're not able to leave a situation. So you have to develop a coping tactic. For example, if your colleague's success stirs up your comparing inner critic, write down what you wish you could feel (*I'm happy for her*) *and* the negative voice inside your head (*She's better than me*). Congratulate her sincerely. Then take one brave step to honor yourself, such as telling a friend who loves you about the statements you wrote, taking a walk to clear your head, or hiring a coach to help you improve a skill.

If you show compassion instead of criticism toward yourself, you'll have a greater capacity to honor the whole range of your feelings. You'll develop the capacity to honor someone else's success even as you invest in your own.

The Guilt Messages of False Humility

As a psychologist and a student of religion, I have spent decades studying the "near enemies" of humility. Whereas a "far enemy" is the opposite of a certain quality, a "near enemy" mimics the genuine virtue but is actually insidious and harmful.[6] For instance, in the case of humility, a far enemy would be arrogance. Most of us want to avoid that. But near enemies of humility—self-deprecation, self-abnegation, and even passivity—show up in many forms, especially in faith communities where they are often celebrated. As I've examined these false versions of humility, both professionally and personally, I've discovered that they can lead to a subtle form of comparison that's often rationalized spiritually.

For years I had a very stubborn voice in my head that was prone to observe and point out excellence in others across almost every category. *She's smarter than me. She's a real athlete, unlike me! Now that's an actual leader!* And the list would go on. I was good at holding up a mirror to reflect the good I saw in others. That wasn't always a bad thing. The problem was that I was honoring the amazing qualities in others while denigrating myself.

And for a long time I thought this was the Christian thing to do. I may have been the paragon of mastering Paul's exhortation to "value others above yourselves."[7] I believed that thinking of others as superior to myself was how God wanted me to be.

I could not have been more wrong. Somehow Paul's exhortation had gotten all twisted up inside my soul. I became so adept at pointing out the strengths of others that I almost completely lost sight of my own. Even as I obtained my fair share of accomplishments, a part of me shrank from owning them. And that part of me rationalized that staying small was somehow what God wanted from me.

This type of thinking is common in our culture, especially for women. You don't want to be arrogant or selfish. So you overcorrect. While it's a beautiful quality to honor and support others, it's not healthy to do it at your own expense. You can honor others *and* honor yourself.[8]

When you internalize a form of false humility, comparison stirs up a wistful longing. You see qualities or gifts in others that you've denied in yourself. You don't want to feel that way, so you rely on guilt messages.

I really shouldn't care about success!

I should just stay small.

I should focus on lifting others up!

If you resonate with any of these guilt messages and notice a genuine longing when comparing yourself to others, consider naming a form of false humility. Then answer some of the following framing questions:

- **Facts:** *What are my gifts and strengths?*
- **Roots:** *Why do I feel guilty about claiming them? When did I learn false humility?*
- **Audit:** *How has playing small served me? How has it hurt me?*
- **Mental Messages:** *What messages do I tell myself about using my gifts? Are they true?*
- **Expansion:** *How does God view my strengths? How might others benefit from them?*

Most of all, consider the possibility that God actually wants more for you!

False humility misses one-half of the truth. It's healthy to honor the gifts in others, yes. *And* you, too, have good gifts; you are unique in every way. Consider the following reframe: **TRUE HUMILITY GOES HAND IN HAND WITH CONFIDENCE.** true humility goes hand in hand with confidence. False humility says, *I don't have as much to offer as other people do.* Confidence says, *I'm good at this. I'm grateful for these* *gifts. I want to use them well.* Confidence is not about superiority or hierarchy—it has nothing to do with comparing yourself to others! It's simply honoring what gifts you have, no matter how big or small they might seem to you. Remember the boy with the loaves and fish in the Bible? He bravely came forth to offer what he had. And God blessed it.[9] As you shift your eyes off others and focus on your own gifts, you'll be surprised at all that God can do through you.

BRAVING CONFIDENCE

Try the following steps as you brave confidence:

- **Identify your strengths and talents:** Consider what you're naturally good at, what you enjoy, and what others compliment you on. If you're feeling uncertain you might use a formal assessment tool, such as StrengthsFinder.[10]
- **Seek input:** Ask trusted friends or coworkers what strengths they see in you.
- **Advance your skills:** Take a class or read a book to help you hone a talent you enjoy.
- **Practice gratitude:** Make a list of three things you're proud of in yourself each day. Write it on a sticky note and put it where you can see it. Give thanks to God for these gifts.

As you take braving steps to honor your own gifts and talents, notice what emotions you feel. If you notice guilt, fear, or discomfort, name those emotions too. It can feel vulnerable to notice and claim your own strengths and talents. But remember your goal isn't to be better than others. Your goal is to become the best version of who *you* are. True humility celebrates the gifts of others *and* delights when you shine your own light.

The Two Sides of Envy

Sometimes comparison is rooted in good old-fashioned envy. You see what somebody else has and you want it. You might even feel entitled to it. It might be that you want the recognition someone else is getting. Or you want their relationships, their financial success, or their happiness.

Envy gets a bad rap and for good reason. I've observed the terrible destruction envy can wreak in the lives of many of my clients and in my friend groups. When envy goes unnamed, it festers and turns into resentment. It leads to a preoccupation with another person, including complex feelings characterized by both love and hate. If unchecked the dissonance of envy can result in a toxic narrative: *She thinks she's so much better than other people.* Or *She's full of herself.* Unchecked envy can prompt gossip, slander, and even malicious, abusive attempts to thwart someone else's success.

On the other hand, when you name envy and face it honestly, it can become a helpful guide, leading you to identify and understand the buried desires or needs that live deep inside you.[11] If you notice envy, don't shame yourself for it. It's a normal human emotion. But do be vigilant to name and frame it so you can brave a healthier mental state.

If you find yourself envying someone, name it, take a deep breath, then ask yourself the following framing questions:

- **Facts:** *What triggers my envy?*
- **Roots:** *What longing or desire is underneath my envy?*
- **Audit:** *What have I done when I felt envy in the past? Did it help?*
- **Mental Messages:** *What messages do I tell myself about envy?*
- **Expansion:** *How might I use this information to motivate myself, instead of envy someone else?*

Then bravely focus on your own path. That's what my client Beth did when she noticed envy. She had been a talented singer leading worship at her church for years. But over time she became unable to perform because of a medical condition that had impaired her vocal cords. As she sat in church every Sunday, she noticed herself feeling envy whenever the worship team came onstage.

As Beth told me about her envy, conflicting emotions reared up from inside her: "I hate myself that I can't just be happy for my friends! Why do I feel this way?"

"It makes sense that you feel envy, Beth," I said. "You've suffered a terrible loss. The fact that you're naming it is such important work. Could we pause here for a moment and consider what longing or need envy is stirring up?"

As Beth shared honestly about her envy in the safety of our relationship, shame lost its grip and grief began to well up. "I miss singing so very much. It just feels like too much to sit in church every Sunday not being a part of it."

As I listened to Beth, I noticed a theme that I've observed in so many others I've counseled. Like many of us, Beth was trying to move too quickly from where she'd been to the place she thought she ought to be. It was as if she was pushing on a bruise that hadn't healed yet. She was trying to "should" herself into being fine. But she wasn't fine. And envy was a cue that she needed to brave the work of tending to her own grief.

Beth wanted to fight for change—she loved her church and didn't want to leave it. But she also wasn't ready to enter back in as if nothing had happened. So she decided to create a place in between for herself and attend a different church—one that wasn't fraught with complicated memories—for a season, so she could grieve her own loss. Beth loved her church, *and* it was triggering a painful, ungrieved loss inside her. She could both honor her friends on the worship team *and* honor the pain that still lived inside her. Over time, as she tended her own grief, she found new ways to reengage and contribute to the faith community she loved so much.

Like Beth, you might need to create space and time to heal the painful comparison that wells up inside you as a result of envy. In other cases you might need to practice suffering envy wisely. For example, it's normal to envy a loved one or friend who has something you long to have. Remember: You can honor the other person *and* honor your own longing. You can acknowledge someone else's good news *and* lament your own disappointment. You can celebrate their success *and* double down on your own aspirations.

Facing envy requires mental rigor. But as you practice naming, framing, and braving envy, you'll not only feel more peaceful toward others, you'll create a better future for yourself.

Lingering Wounds of Self-Doubt

Sometimes wounds from the past keep us stuck in negative comparison. If you were neglected by your parents, bullied by peers, or simply struggled to find your own voice amid a sea of others, you may struggle with deeply seated self-doubts, fears, or insecurities. Part of you yearns to live into the fullness of life you see other people enjoying, but you may not be able to gather the confidence or courage to do it. As a result, you stay stuck in a mental loop of longing for change but doubting your capacity to achieve it.

At its most extreme, unhealthy comparison stems from a lack of mirroring in childhood. You might not have been taught how to form your own self-concept: to reflect on and evaluate your own life, character, and accomplishments. As a result, you're constantly looking toward other people to assess and validate yourself. In some faith communities you're taught that you *should* look outside of yourself, that you're not a trustworthy source of information about how to shape your own life. But while it's wise to look to God and trusted friends for guidance, it's also crucial that you look to resources within yourself—including your God-given longings, strengths, and talents—as you navigate your own life.

As I worked with my client Erin, we began to name self-doubt as the root of her tendency to compare her life to the lives of others. Unhealed pain from her past was shaping her current thoughts. Her parents were active and present in her life on a superficial level but completely absent emotionally and mentally. They hadn't held up a mirror and helped her name beautiful aspects of herself: "Erin, I see this quality in you." They hadn't helped her figure out how to cultivate her gifts and strengths. A part of her had coped with neglect by fixating on the accomplishments of everyone around her. Now it was as if a young girl inside Erin was still looking around, asking *Is that who I should be?* or *If I was more like her, would my parents finally notice me?*

As we framed her self-doubt, Erin realized that the scope of her comparison issue was deep—she was going to need to do more than simply "get off social media and learn to be content," as her mom had suggested. Instead, she was going to need to brave the work of healing, including setting boundaries with the part of her that focused on others, finding activities that reflected her interests, and asserting her own voice into her relationships.

Through our work together Erin began to observe and notice the unique constellation of gifts and longings God had placed inside her. She stopped looking to others to define who she was, and she began to see herself as God does—a beautiful soul created to bear his image in this life in a unique and wonderful way.

NAME, FRAME, AND BRAVE COMPARISON

Name: Recall a recent situation that evoked a negative feeling of comparison in you.

Frame: What messages are you telling yourself about this situation?

- Are you self-critical? (*I should have been better.*)

- Do you notice guilt messages? (*I shouldn't feel this way.*)
- Do you feel envy? (*I want what they have.*)
- Do you notice self-doubt? (*I'll never be good enough.*)

Write a holy reframe for each message you notice.

- *I wasn't my best,* **and** *I can learn and grow from this experience.*
- *I can honor their happiness,* **and** *I can honor my sadness.*
- *I can acknowledge their success,* **and** *I can clarify the good things I want.*
- *I'm not where I want to be,* **and** *I'm precious to God as I am.*

Brave: Identify and take one proactive step to invest in your own dream, growth, or God-given longing.

A Twofold Solution

I can promise you one thing: problems with social comparison do not discriminate; everyone compares themselves to other people. The solution to the problem of comparison, once you recognize how it shows up in your life, is to honor what's legitimately frustrating *and* take brave steps to focus on developing your own gifts.

Consider a pendulum that swings back and forth. If you swing too far toward dwelling on what you don't have in comparison to others, you risk self-pity, envy, or victimization. On the other hand, if you swing too far toward force-fitting contentment, you risk deceiving yourself with shallow platitudes or toxic positivity. Neither extreme works.

In contrast to the wild swings of a pendulum, a plumb line helps you stay aligned vertically with God, the one who knows you best. A plumb line is a magnetically weighted vertical line that extends directly toward the center of gravity. Painters and woodworkers use plumb lines to keep their lines straight. The term appears in the Bible several times, but one of the most notable places is in the book of Amos when God's people were so focused on gaining material success—trying to be better than their peers—that they were taking advantage of the sick, the poor, and the vulnerable. In a vivid gesture, God held up a plumb line to show them how far they had strayed from aligning their ways to his.[12] They were no longer seeking God's direction. They had swung completely away from him.

We can also use the idea of a plumb line in our own lives. Developing a vertical plumb line between yourself and God helps you stay true to your own experience *and* aligned with the one who made you. You stop gauging your own success or making decisions based on looking out horizontally to other people. That doesn't mean you ignore or bypass what's hard as you survey the landscape around you. Instead, it means you name those feelings—self-criticism, guilt, envy, or self-doubt—then, with God's help, work to align them with what's true.

Naming what's hard as a form of prayer is a powerful practice to help you stay aligned with God's heart.

It's hard to see the way other marriages are thriving when mine is not. God, help me be wise about my own marriage.

It's hard to struggle financially when my friends are not. God, help me focus on my own next steps.

It's hard to feel lonely when others seem so happy. God, help me focus on what I can do to cultivate meaningful relationships.

Remember: two things can be true. As you name what's hard *and* what's in your control, you surrender to a fuller picture of your situation. You stop dwelling on someone else's circumstances and start focusing on your own path. You ask God to join you in shaping your own reality. In this practice of relentless honesty, your mind calms. Your resolve strengthens.

AS YOU NAME WHAT'S HARD *AND* WHAT'S IN YOUR CONTROL, YOU SURRENDER TO A FULLER PICTURE OF YOUR SITUATION.

You gain freedom from the false messages you've carried, and you build trust with God and with yourself. You discover the joy and deep satisfaction of taking charge of your own life and nurturing your talents. You take brave steps toward what you actually need and want, instead of comparing yourself to others.

PART THREE

I Shouldn't Feel This Way About Others

NINE

I Shouldn't Feel Trapped in Toxicity

Sarah met Matt nearly a year after going through a painful divorce. Matt had a fun-loving personality, and his attention was irresistible. The two became inseparable, forging a deep bond during an otherwise lonely season. As their romance blossomed over the next year, they began to make plans for a future together.

Over time, though, Sarah found herself growing increasingly restless. And Matt seemed to be growing increasingly controlling. While Sarah was starting to enjoy an expanded circle of friends and work that she loved, Matt was becoming increasingly unhappy and increasingly jealous of Sarah's new friends and fulfilling career.

When Sarah came to see me, she was at her wits' end. "I don't know what to do," she said. "Matt was there for me through a really hard time when we first met. Shouldn't I be grateful to him for that?

I'm his best friend. He doesn't have anyone else. But I'm just not sure I can continue on like this."

As Sarah began to name the confusion she felt inside, I wondered if there was more to the situation than her fear of hurting someone. I decided to ask a question to determine whether Sarah needed to learn assertiveness or if there was something more complex about this situation.

"Sarah, have you tried letting Matt know that you have concerns about the relationship?"

"I can't," Sarah said. "That would be impossible."

"I'm confused, Sarah," I reflected. "What happens when you try to raise your concerns with Matt?"

"I've tried to tell him I need more space, that I'm feeling suffocated. But he doesn't seem to hear me. He just says I don't know how good I have it. That we both know it's God's will for us to be together. That I have problems with commitment."

"So if you raise concerns about your relationship, Matt suggests you're defying God's will or that you're being noncommittal?" I asked, trying to keep my voice neutral.

"Yes," Sarah said. "But, I mean, I've agreed with him on that. I've told him how much God has used him in my life. And I *have* struggled with making commitments in the past. Matt says that's exactly why I need him. My friends can't figure out why I don't just leave him, but it's not that simple for me."

Matt was clearly not respecting Sarah's sincere attempt to raise a legitimate concern. Instead of listening and working to address her concerns, he was using toxic strategies to try to get her to doubt herself. He was also using God to further amplify his authority in her life. I understood why Sarah felt so confused. Sarah had a kind heart, and Matt had done an expert job of using toxic strategies to capitalize on her empathy and evoke guilt to keep her stuck.

Like Sarah, you might be in a relationship with someone who demonstrates a pattern of toxic behaviors over time. Leaving such relationships can be complicated. There might be financial implications. You might share children with that person. The toxicity might be coming from a parent or sibling or close family member— someone to whom you feel a sense of responsibility. It might be coming from your own adult child. These situations are not easy to navigate, in part because the other person knows how to exploit the guilt messages already running through your mind.

Please hear me when I say this: toxic strategies are designed to keep you feeling confused, stuck, and doubtful of yourself. Please do not beat yourself up for feeling these ways! Instead, you can equip yourself to disentangle from toxicity and brave the health and goodness you deserve. Whether you fight for change, leave the relationship, or decide to suffer parts of it wisely—for whatever reason—you can find your way out of toxicity one brave step at a time.

Why Name Toxicity?

I wish I didn't have to devote an entire chapter of this book to toxicity. But I've lived too long and seen too much not to know the magnitude of this problem. Sometimes doing the brave work of naming means you will have to label a behavior as "toxic." There is just no other name that will do. Imagine if you were to ingest a toxic substance—you'd need to identify the exact nature of the substance so that poison control professionals could help you remove it from your system and prevent ongoing harm. The same is true with toxic behaviors. When you name them accurately, you can work to neutralize their harmful impact and take wise steps to limit exposure going forward.

Not all negative behaviors are toxic. For example, it's normal to feel angry with or hurt by someone you love. A loving spouse still misunderstands you sometimes. Your children behave in ways that disappoint you. Even the best of friends let you down. Your parents frustrate you. Each of us can be toxic in a moment. We can lie, deceive, manipulate, guilt-message, control, or criticize. We can bully and blame shift. We can lose our tempers and lash out at others. We can act self-centered or arrogant. We are human. We make mistakes. We succumb to the worst of ourselves at times. There's a difference between someone who's toxic in a moment and someone who demonstrates a consistent, pervasive pattern of toxic behaviors—a recurring set of actions that happen over time.

In healthy relationships people take responsibility for their missteps. They make amends. Each person does their own work of naming their mistakes, framing them, and braving hard conversations when they are necessary. When both parties engage this process, ruptures lead to repair that yields deeper understanding, the sweet balm of forgiveness, and clearer strategies for moving forward. Unfortunately, this is not always what happens.

When one person in the relationship heads down the path of toxicity, that person disrupts and harms the normal processes required to sustain and grow a healthy bond. These individuals hurt you, and they don't name their own hurtful choices. Or even if they do name them, they don't take responsibility for them; instead, they blame you or other people. They consistently create roadblocks to healthy communication; they might manipulate the truth, guilt-trip, lie, gaslight, or refuse to communicate altogether. When you confront their behavior, they contaminate any mechanism by which repair might be possible. They might even double down and attempt to hurt you more.

It's therefore not safe to express normal concerns, frustration, or even hurt to someone who is treating you in a toxic way. Those emotions are vulnerable. You need safety in order to share when you're hurt or angry with someone you love. But someone who is toxic is the opposite of safe. They will take those vulnerable emotions and use them against you.

This is why it's so important to name toxic behaviors for what they are. When you don't understand the nature of toxicity, you inadvertently put yourself in harm's way. For example, you might attempt to raise a legitimate concern only to be met with lies, manipulation, or a guilt message. You get confused, and you might doubt or blame yourself: *Am I the problem here?* You might tell yourself you must have done something to deserve this mistreatment: *It must be my fault.* Or you might question why you can't simply feel peace inside: *Maybe I just need to try harder and be more loving.*

Whereas life-giving behaviors inspire positive qualities—love, joy, peace, patience, kindness, goodness, faithfulness, gentleness, and self-control[1]—in oneself and others, toxic behaviors have the exact opposite effect. Toxic behaviors leave you feeling trapped, guilt-ridden, anxious, ashamed, angry, hopeless, and confused, even though a part of you is aware that you're not doing anything wrong. Recognizing and naming a toxic strategy can help you take brave steps to neutralize it and protect yourself from further harm.

Naming Toxic Behaviors

Toxic behaviors stem from an effort to exert control or power over others. Instead of taking ownership of one's own issue or viewpoint, a person uses toxic strategies to try to control or manipulate someone else. In its simplest form, toxicity starts like this: *I don't like the way I feel inside. I'll attempt to soothe my own stress or pain by manipulating my external environment—including other people—to make myself feel better.*

Humans move toward growth or decay. A pattern of toxic choices over time leads to decay—alienation from the best of someone's God-made self, making it nearly impossible for that person to genuinely love and honor other people.

Toxic behaviors can manifest in many ways, ranging from minor violations to abusive, violent actions. Such behaviors include control, manipulation, bullying, gaslighting, coercion, blame shifting, and emotional, physical, sexual, or psychological abuse. The bottom line when it comes to toxic behaviors is that the other person isn't trying to help you, even when they pretend that they are. They're trying to harm or control you to serve their own interests.

Here are some of the most common types of toxic behaviors to be on the lookout for.

Control and Manipulation

Typically, people who are adept at controlling or manipulating others know how to capitalize on another person's areas of vulnerability. They'll take advantage of a tender heart, an empathetic spirit, or a loyal nature and exploit those qualities. They might do this in direct, overt ways by dictating to you the way you should think or act.

For example, a controlling spouse might refuse to let his partner have access to financial information to keep her dependent on him. A parent might establish rigid rules in an attempt to control a child's behavior. A friend or significant other might try to control someone by telling her what she should wear or whom she should hang out with. Overtly controlling statements sound like this:

- "You need to do it my way."
- "I know what's best for you."
- "You're not capable of handling this on your own."
- "I don't want you to associate with those people."
- "I'm doing this for your own good."
- "You couldn't survive without me."

Someone might also try to control your behavior in more indirect, covert ways through various forms of manipulation. For example, a parent might guilt-message you by constantly bringing up all the sacrifices they've made on your behalf. A friend or family member might try to manipulate you by crying, giving you the silent treatment, or growing angry if you say a healthy no to them. A faith community might try to get you to give money by using spiritual manipulation: "God would want you to make that sacrifice!" Manipulative statements sound like this:

- "I've given everything for you."
- "I guess you're just too busy for me."
- "If you really loved me, you would . . ."
- "If you really loved God, you would . . ."
- "You're the only one I have."
- "Can you please just do this one thing for me?" (And the "one thing" in this case is something toxic.)

Triangulation

Triangulation occurs when one person pulls you into the middle of a conflict with a third person. Instead of working through the problem directly with the other person, individuals who triangulate will use or manipulate you. They might dump their frustration on you but never address it with the other person, try to coerce you into going to the other person so that they don't have to, or share damaging information about the other person in an attempt to gain your trust.

Triangulation is especially toxic when parents do it to a child. A parent might confide in you about your other parent's flaws in an attempt to get you to align with them against the other. Or a parent might share with you how your sibling hurt them, in an attempt to get you to coerce your sibling into apologizing. It's a parent's job to help a child feel safe and protected and to normalize healthy conflict, such as by saying "Your dad and I don't always agree. But what's most important is that we love you. Our conflict is never your fault or your responsibility!"

Triangulation traps you in the middle, which creates dissonance and turmoil inside. You want to help your friend or family member. The problem is you've been put in the middle of a problem that you don't have the power to solve. You absorb all the weight or pain of the conflict without any clear path to resolve it. When it occurs consistently over time, you do not get the attention and support you deserve. You're viewed as a dumping ground for other people's problems instead of as your own distinct person who is worthy of care and respect.

If you've experienced triangulation, you're likely deeply acquainted with the uncomfortable mix of anxiety, guilt, and helplessness that comes from being placed in the middle of other people's problems. But when you recognize what's happening and name triangulation for what it is, you can take action to stop it from happening by asserting yourself: "I'd prefer you talk to that person directly!" Or you can set a healthy boundary: "If you bring this person up again, I'll remove myself from the conversation."

Finally, it's important to note that there are healthy ways to seek third-party counsel from other adults that do not involve triangulation. You can do this by following these three steps:

1. **Name what's happening:** "I need some advice about a hard situation."
2. **Ask permission:** "Are you available, and do you have the capacity to help me?"
3. **Clarify the boundaries:** "I'm not asking you to fix this. I'm

asking for you to help me see it clearly so that I can take steps to resolve the situation."

Blame Shifting

When individuals blame shift, they put the blame on someone else for their problems instead of taking responsibility themselves. For example, a parent might blame a child for their mental illness: "If you weren't so poorly behaved, I wouldn't be so depressed!" A coworker might consistently blame others for his poor performance: "I only did it that way because she told me to!" Or a spouse might blame his partner for his own poor choices: "It's your fault that I drink so much."

Blame shifting creates a confusing atmosphere of half-truths and deception, making it hard to discern what's real. At face value these excuses seem to have merit. For example, maybe you did behave poorly in that moment. But over time you start to see a pattern emerge and you can name it: "Oh, I get it. There's always someone else to blame!" The truth is that each of us has to take responsibility for our own behaviors. Blaming others never helps.

Verbal Abuse

Verbal abuse includes the use of derogatory language, insults, or threats to belittle or degrade someone. This might include name-calling, cruel manipulation, or fear-and-intimidation tactics to control you. Here are some examples:

- "You're a [fill in the derogatory word here]."

- "If you leave, I'll make sure you regret it."
- "I'm sure our friends would love to know about your shameful secrets."

A more indirect form of verbal abuse is constant criticism. When someone continually undermines you, points out perceived flaws, or criticizes your actions, appearance, or abilities, it's toxic. When you're the target of constant criticism, it's as if you are receiving a million tiny paper cuts to your soul. Criticism can show up with shaming comments, sarcasm, or insults, such as in the following statements:

- "You're always so disorganized. Can't you do anything right?"
- "Are you really going to wear *that*?"
- "As if you'd ever offer to help." (Said with eye-rolling.)
- "Not everyone can be as perfect as you, can they?" (Said with sarcasm.)

These comments leave you feeling wounded. Constant exposure erodes your confidence and leads to feelings of helplessness, as if you can't do anything right. You were not created to thrive in a toxic environment that is cruel, shaming, or harsh. You need and deserve warmth, loving care, and compassion—we all do! If you've been trapped in a situation where you are constantly criticized, please know you are worth so much more than that. Take steps to seek and find those places where you receive the good, kind, healing words your heart and soul deserve.

Gaslighting

Gaslighting is a form of psychological abuse in which your reality or experience is systematically and intentionally invalidated. Someone manipulates you by questioning your words or your perception of reality—their goal is to make you feel crazy, weak, or dependent. Make no mistake: a gaslighter is not questioning you to help you or as a collaborative effort to arrive at shared truth. Gaslighters question you to gain power over you.

Gaslighting involves two components: deception and projection. Gaslighters lie to protect themselves, then go on the attack to disempower you. For example, your spouse starts drinking again, and you confront him. He might say "I'm not drinking—you're paranoid!" when he is, in fact, drinking again. He's lied about his behavior, and he's turned the accusation onto you.

Gaslighting is particularly dangerous if you call someone out for their toxic ways. For example, let's say you attempt to set a healthy boundary with someone who has been slandering you. Instead of owning up to the behavior, they deny it and go on the attack: "I never said those things—you're being toxic!" This type of victim blaming is an atrocity: it retraumatizes the person who experienced the injury in the first place.

A PERSON WHO USES TOXIC STRATEGIES HAS NOT EARNED THE PRIVILEGE OF YOUR PRESENCE.

If you're in a relationship with someone who gaslights, words will not work; they'll be spun and used against you. Resist attempts to explain yourself or get them to understand you. Then, with the support of those who love and honor you, take steps to remove yourself from exposure. A person who uses toxic strategies has not earned the privilege of your presence.

Physical or Sexual Abuse

Physical abuse is the intentional use of physical force to hurt, intimidate, punish, or threaten another person. It includes actions like hitting, slapping, punching, choking, or any form of physical aggression. It might result in injury, but even if it doesn't cause observable injury, it creates a gash to the soul.

Sexual abuse refers to any type of nonconsensual sexual contact or behavior. It can range from inappropriate comments or innuendo to touching, rape, or exploitation of a person for the purpose of sexual gratification. Someone who is abusing you might use phrases such as "Don't tell anyone, but . . . ," "It's our little secret," "No one would believe you anyway," or "I know you want this." It can occur in families, in marriages, at work, or at church. Please hear me say: It is not your fault. You do not invite sexual abuse; other people perpetrate it.

If you're in a relationship with someone who is abusing you in any way, please seek support. Your mind, your heart, your soul, and your body are worthy of dignity and respect, and you deserve so much more! There are numerous support groups, including 24-7 hotlines with smart, kindhearted people trained to get you to a safe, healing place.[2]

It's confusing when someone controls, manipulates, or abuses you in any of these ways. You're not wired to expect such treatment from other people. You're wired for love and connection. Toxicity often stirs up guilt, anxiety, and fear. Please be gentle with yourself as you consider your own situation. It's easy to get caught up in the web of words another person spins, especially if it's someone you thought you could trust. When you work to identify and name toxic behaviors, seek out the support of a naming partner—a therapist, trusted friend, or support group—who can help you name what's happening clearly.

Identifying and naming toxicity often brings some relief in and of itself. When you understand what you're dealing with, you can move out of the haze of second-guessing yourself and into a clearer place in your mind. Next, take the time you need to frame the situation and create a strategy to brave your way out of toxicity and into the life you were made to enjoy.

Framing Toxic Behaviors

Toxic behaviors lie on a spectrum, and they have different degrees of impact. For example, some toxic behaviors are relatively isolated. You may have a mother-in-law who triangulates with you about her son, your spouse. You don't like it, and she won't stop. But you can set boundaries with the behavior and still enjoy her good qualities. Or you might have a spouse who criticizes your parenting. He can't name the pattern in himself, and it's challenging for you to live with. On the other hand, he also demonstrates love and care in other ways. In such cases you can work to quarantine the behavior and still enjoy other aspects of the relationship.

Some toxic behaviors develop into pervasive patterns, creating a large impact. The negative effect far outweighs any benefit. In such cases you might need to reduce the amount of time you spend with this person or remove yourself from the relationship altogether. If you're experiencing toxicity, ask yourself some of the following questions to help you frame the impact:

- **Facts:** *How often does the behavior occur? When does it occur?*
- **Roots:** *When did the behaviors start? How did I respond to the behaviors initially?*
- **Audit:** *Have I tried to address the behaviors? What happened?*
- **Mental Messages:** *Do I frequently feel uncomfortable, belittled, or drained after time with this person? What guilt or shame messages do I tell myself?*
- **Expansion:** *Have others in my life mentioned concerns about this person's behavior? What do experts say about the behaviors?*

You can also use the Looking Tool to assess the big picture of your relationship:

- **Looking Back:** *Have I ever experienced a healthy relationship with this person? If so, what were the circumstances?*
- **Looking at Today:** *On a scale from 1 to 10, how content am I with the current relationship? What fears do I have about changing how I show up in this relationship?*
- **Looking Ahead:** *What would progress look like one year, five*

years, or ten years from now? What decisions would I regret one year, five years, or ten years from now?

When you take the time to frame the toxicity, you'll gain clarity. Remember my client Sarah who was experiencing toxicity with Matt? As I worked with her to help her frame her situation, she began to see that he had shown patterns of control since they'd first met. In fact, she recalled him describing a prior breakup. He had placed all the blame on his ex for not respecting him and frequently spoke of her in disparaging terms. But as Sarah looked back, she realized that might not have been the whole picture. She couldn't think of a time in their relationship when Matt hadn't blamed others for his actions. She began to realize there was indeed a clear pattern of blame shifting—this wasn't an isolated problem.

As you frame toxic behaviors, you'll begin to ascertain whether this is a relationship you wish to fight for or a relationship you need to leave behind. Finally, in some cases, you may determine that you'll need to find ways to suffer it wisely. Regardless, it's time to take brave action.

Braving Boundaries with Toxicity

Your goal when dealing with toxic behaviors is to take effective action to remove yourself from the toxicity as much as possible while maintaining your own safety and sanity. Many people get fixated on wanting to get the other person to change or at least understand what they've done wrong. I get it. It's painful to watch someone choose to continue in their toxic ways. But the bottom line is that you can't change another person. You can only take charge of your own responses and actions. The best thing you can do is to brave your own path toward health.

Regardless of whether you decide to fight for change, leave the relationship, or suffer it wisely, consider taking brave steps in each of the following categories:

- **Boundaries:** excuse yourself from a toxic conversation
- **Range:** practice grounding exercises before entering into a conversation with a toxic person
- **Assertiveness:** create a script and practice it (see below for examples)
- **Vitality:** celebrate a holiday with people you love and enjoy
- **Environment:** schedule weekly support with positive and encouraging people

Please note: people will often encourage you to jump to setting boundaries before you are ready to do so. You may need to first build up your support network, strengthen your voice, or replenish already depleted emotional reserves before you're ready to set a boundary. Pay attention to your own inner wisdom as you take brave steps to remove toxicity from your life and relationships.

Fighting for Change

In some cases you may decide to fight for change. As a result of framing, you see benefits to keeping the relationship *and* you need to take steps to remove yourself from a toxic behavior. To be clear, this doesn't mean you're fighting to change the other person. It means you're fighting for the relationship through changing *your* behaviors. Your goal is to create a boundary between yourself and the toxic behavior. And you can do this with your words, actions, or both.

Word boundaries are communicated verbally or in writing. You tell the other person how you're going to change your behavior in response to a toxic behavior. Here are some guidelines as you specify this kind of boundary:

- Fewer words are clearer.
- Affirm the good.
- Name the toxic behavior.
- Identify your action step.

Remember: the goal of a word boundary is to state the action *you* are going to take. Your boundary should be something you can implement without their help, permission, or consent. Here are some examples of how to set a healthy word boundary:

- "I appreciate you and value our relationship. I've noticed that our conversations often veer into discussing your issues with [insert name of third person here]. This triangulation is uncomfortable, and it stirs up anxiety inside me. In the future I'll be steering clear of such discussions or ending the conversation if it continues. I'm not going to discuss this person with you."
- "I've been thinking about our recent interactions, and I've

noticed there's been a pattern of shifting blame onto me. I am more than willing to be here for you. But I'll provide that support only when you're ready to take responsibility for your own behaviors. Until then I won't be engaging in conversations about this topic."

- "I want you to enjoy the kids, but I'm not going to listen to your criticism of me anymore. If you criticize me again, I'll hang up the phone or leave the room. I'm happy to give you updates about what the kids are learning at school, but that's where the conversation ends."

Then back up your words with actions.

Action boundaries are communicated through changes in your behaviors. Instead of using words to communicate, you simply refuse to engage. You might use the grounding exercises in chapter 7 to calm your nervous system in a tricky situation. For example, maybe you take one long deep breath when someone tries to criticize or guilt-message you. Then you might turn and walk away. Or imagine a soothing place in your mind when someone flips into a blame-shifting monologue. Then change the topic of conversation. You might leave the room when the toxic behavior occurs or excuse yourself from the phone if an inappropriate topic comes up. You do not owe the other person an explanation. When you stay grounded in your body and emotionally regulated—and refuse to take the bait—you show strength and conviction.

Remember: these word and action boundaries are designed to help you cope in relationships that you've deemed "good enough" to fight for. As you take charge of your own reactions, you transform the dynamics of a relationship. When you extract yourself from a toxic cycle, you not only empower yourself but also pave the way for the other person to discover and adopt a healthier approach.

Leaving the Relationship

In other cases you might need to leave a relationship altogether. You've poured yourself out, but they're not changing and every attempt to communicate gets weaponized and used against you. It's time to remove yourself from the relationship.

There might be a time when there is no need to communicate your decision. You've already tried. Your goal is to close the door to further contact in whatever way is necessary. In other cases you may want to convey what you have decided. The goal is not to open up a two-way conversation. You've made your decision. Instead, you're simply providing closure. Keep it brief. "I'm no longer going to invest in this relationship. I need to focus on my own health [or on other relationships]. My hope is for both of us to find the peace and happiness we deserve."

If you communicate this decision in person, be sure to have a clear exit strategy so that you can leave quickly if the conversation becomes toxic. You might meet in a public place, such as a park or coffee shop. It's also wise to ask a third party, such as a therapist, friend, or family member, to be present in case the other person attempts to entangle you in a war of words.

Then back up this decision with your actions. Stop responding to any text, phone call, or email they might send you. Block their phone number, access to your social media, and email address if necessary. Discard physical mail or give it to the police if it contains any form of threat. If you see them in public, you can acknowledge their humanity with a civil greeting, but that's where communication ends.

As Sarah framed her situation with Matt, she was initially conflicted. A part of her felt fearful to break up with him. She knew that Matt would not take it well: he would blame her and likely paint an ugly picture of her to their mutual acquaintances. She also realized that the very fact he would do this meant she could not stay in a relationship with him. As a result of her time in the place in between, her braving steps became clear: she set a time and a place to break up with Matt. She then scheduled "sandwich support" for herself—time with two of her friends before and after the breakup conversation to help her stay brave.

Ending a relationship is never simple. But it can paradoxically mark the beginning of a path toward healing. When you release the other person and their actions to God, you can begin to focus on your own well-being. You free yourself to live a life of renewed purpose and peace.

Neutralizing Impact When You Can't Leave

In some instances you can't leave a relationship; you have to suffer it wisely. This might occur when you are caring for an aging family member or co-parenting your children with an ex. Here are some examples of proactive steps you can take to neutralize the impact of toxic behaviors in such situations:

- Stop spending time alone with the person. Use the buddy system or meet in public.

- Set a time limit. Pre-commit to a specific amount of time you will spend when you have to be at a gathering with this person.
- Change communication channels. Switch to written communication, such as email versus phone calls.
- Preselect topics of conversation. Make a list of neutral or safe topics of conversation and stick to them. Don't share details about your private life, thoughts, or feelings.
- Appoint a third party. Use an intermediary to convey essential information to and from the other person.

Remember: braving has some trial and error to it. You may start down one of these paths only to realize you need to make an adjustment. The other person may surprise you in positive ways. Or they might surprise you by showing more toxicity than you suspected. It's wise to stay alert and nimble as you implement your plan. Dealing with toxic behaviors is not about a tidy process of communication; it's about getting a safe outcome.

Toxic strategies are designed to control or manipulate you.

DEALING WITH TOXIC BEHAVIORS IS NOT ABOUT A TIDY PROCESS OF COMMUNICATION; IT'S ABOUT GETTING A SAFE OUTCOME.

When you refuse to engage with them, you send a powerful message about your God-given agency. The other person can try to harm you, but they can't take away your dignity or your worth. Brave resistance to toxicity is what I believe Jesus meant when he used the phrase "turn the other cheek."[3]

Shrewd and Innocent

Years ago, I had to name and brave boundaries with an extremely controlling friend. Initially I had admired her decisiveness and strong opinions. But as our relationship progressed, it became clear that she had strong ideas of who she thought I should be and the passions she thought I should pursue. She grew increasingly controlling of me to the point where I was starting to hide aspects of my life from her, including other friendships, to avoid her rage and jealousy. At the same time, I cared about this person, and there were good things about our relationship.

As time went on, I realized that the problem wasn't going to cure itself. To fight for our relationship, I was going to have to speak up about what was happening. So I set a time and a place to meet.

Chaotic thoughts and feelings flew through my mind. *But I've done things wrong too. I've enabled her in so many ways. I've told her what she wanted to hear.* Well-meaning friends tried to remind me that her choices weren't my fault. I knew this was true, but I also saw my own culpability in the situation. After all, I'd participated in our dynamic.

A few days before our conversation, I stumbled upon one of my favorite passages in the Bible, Isaiah 6:1–8, where the prophet struggled with his own inner tensions. Isaiah was about to be used by God to name atrocities and toxic behaviors all around him. Even though by all accounts Isaiah was a good and decent man, when confronted with God's holiness Isaiah didn't proudly nominate himself as God's chosen one. Instead, he lamented his own imperfections and acknowledged the collective toxicity of his society.

Isaiah faced his own human brokenness *and* bravely stepped forth to become a Namer of toxicity.

I certainly wasn't being called to do what Isaiah did, but there was something in this passage that settled me. It rang true to my own experience, to the thoughts I'd been wrestling with. Instead of trying to talk myself out of those feelings of guilt, I decided to honor them. *I, too, have not been perfect, God, and that doesn't mean I should continue to put up with her mistreatment of me.*

The wholeness of truth settles us. There's a strange freedom in it. When we confront our own human failings and misdeeds, we paradoxically become more equipped to stand up to toxic behavior when we see it in other people.

When the day of our conversation arrived, I sat down with my friend, my heart heavy but my resolve unwavering. It was awkward. I didn't say everything perfectly. She didn't take it very well. But braving that step gave me a glimpse of the freedom that comes when you align your actions with reality. My soul felt lighter, freer, clearer. I didn't want to hurt my friend, but I could no longer enable her at the expense of my own health.

Naming what's hard is an act of love, a gift you give not only to yourself but also to others. Whether or not the other person recognizes that gift is beside the point. Naming creates an opportunity for both parties—yourself and the other person—to brave a different path. You release the other person to make their own choices. And you free *yourself* to pursue the healing and goodness that lies ahead.

- You can love someone **and** leave a relationship.
- You can forgive someone **and** maintain firm boundaries.

- You can value someone **and** refuse to engage in their toxicity.

Jesus said, "Be wise as serpents and innocent as doves."[4] We long to embody the purity of doves, soaring above life's challenges uncontaminated and free. The problem is that while we are inhabiting this world, we also have to navigate the complexities, at times inching our way through the murky and chaotic underbelly of life. Pretending otherwise won't change reality. Be wise, *and* don't lose your innocence.

As you recognize and name toxicity for what it is, you *will* find your way through it. You *will* move out of its snare and into the healing, the honesty, the loving mutuality God wants for you. And you *will* appreciate the joy of that real love and genuine goodness all the more for the pain you've endured. You'll start to understand why Solomon said that love is as strong as death.[5]

TEN

I Shouldn't Feel Mad at My Loved One

"I'm such a monster!" Isabella exclaimed. "I keep fantasizing about changing the lock on my door and shutting off my phone!"

Isabella said these words to me during a counseling session as tears welled up in her eyes. A wife and the mother of four kids, one of whom struggled with depression, Isabella lived down the street from her sister, who was raising four young children by herself since her husband had left her. Isabella's dad also lived nearby. Widowed and lonely, he showed up at Isabella's house frequently throughout the week.

Isabella protested, "How can I feel this way about my family? My sister has so much on her plate. My dad is alone. My own child is battling depression. What kind of monster would I be to tell them I'm not available?"

She was in a tough spot. Legitimate needs—including her

own—surrounded her every day, and she was starting to break down from the overwhelm. Isabella's desire to lock her door and turn off her phone was her *I shouldn't feel this way* moment—a cue that she needed to spend some time at the Crossroads. She was so aware of what was hard for everybody else that she was losing sight of her own needs. If she didn't stop to navigate the complexity, one of two things would happen:

1. She would continue to live as she had been, neglect her own needs, and jeopardize her health.
2. She would grow resentful and jeopardize her relationships with her family members.

Neither of these options was a good one. So I began the process of helping Isabella name, frame, and brave her way through a complicated situation.

We *all* experience mixed feelings toward our loved ones at times. And our loved ones experience mixed feelings toward us. On one hand, we wish we didn't have to feel this way. On the other hand, those feelings—when named and framed—help us brave a healthier way forward for the benefit of everyone.

Barriers to Relational Health

Anyone who is worthy of your respect and your time has the potential to stir up complicated emotions inside you. You might admire a friend, yet envy her success. You might love your spouse's good qualities and also feel hurt by those same qualities. You might adore your kids and need space from them.

But when you don't know how to work through complicated feelings, you tend to get stuck. You might try to suppress your frustration, because you don't want to hurt anyone. You soldier on with pleasing others, wearing yourself out. Meanwhile, a part of you quietly seethes, feeling frustrated and overlooked.

Why can't my kids just leave me alone?

When will my friend actually check in on me?

I wish my spouse would give me a break.

Why can't my parents just go away?

I'm such a terrible person for feeling this way!

You attempt to shove aside your anger. Silence your disappointment. Shut down your regret. But those unaddressed feelings will find their way out somehow: they'll either wreak havoc inside you or they'll eventually grow so big that they erupt. Instead of working through the conflict, you'll have created an even bigger problem.

Here are some examples of complex feelings you might face:

- You love your deeply feeling, introspective teen, and sometimes he worries you. You don't want to pry, but you also hate feeling shut out.
- Your mom is always willing to babysit, but as a result, she's also always in your space. You feel suffocated by her presence, yet you feel guilty because of all she's doing to help you.
- You fell in love with your partner because of his work ethic. You admire his discipline. As time goes on, you've begun to

notice that this discipline comes with a cost: he often works long hours and doesn't help out much when he finally does come home.

- Your spouse has a good heart and works hard to be a good dad, but his idea of a good conversation is to dissect the latest baseball statistics. You feel agitated and bored, and you notice you're avoiding conversations with him.

- You love your globe-trotting friend and appreciate the ways she inspires your sense of adventure. But the more she shares with you about her travels, the more insecure you feel about your own life—and envious of hers.

- Your sister doesn't care what other people will think of her. You love her boisterous approach to life and devil-may-care attitude. Yet sometimes she hurts or embarrasses you.

How do you navigate these complicated situations? Do you avoid them? Or do you brave hard conversations? If you decide to brave a hard conversation, how do you do it?

None of us becomes equipped to handle relational complexities overnight. And in the absence of instruction on how to navigate relational conflict, we tend to default to our conditioned ways of coping and survival. We create barriers instead of throughways. The first step to relational health is to recognize and name the barriers we all unintentionally put up. Healthy relationships start inside you as you work through your own thinking traps.

HEALTHY RELATIONSHIPS START INSIDE YOU AS YOU WORK THROUGH YOUR OWN THINKING TRAPS.

Assumptions and Mind Reading

Instead of giving other people an opportunity to speak on their own behalf, you make assumptions about their motives or attempt to read their mind. When you mind read, you jump to conclusions about what other people are thinking or feeling without actually knowing what they are thinking or feeling. Even worse, you may take actions based on your mind reading, actions that completely miscalculate the reality of the situation. Here are some examples of how you might do this:

- Your son appears moody at the dinner table. You assume he's upset about his girlfriend, and you anxiously analyze the situation with your spouse. "I just don't think she's good for him!" The truth is your son is completely happy with his girlfriend. He's actually worried about his college admissions applications and doesn't know how to ask for help.
- You assume that your mom spends so much time at your house because she's lonely. You don't want to hurt her feelings, so you don't say anything about your growing feelings of suffocation. The truth is she'd love to spend more time at home, but she thinks you need her help.
- You assume that your spouse isn't interested in your hobbies, that he's selfish. The truth is he doesn't know how to ask you questions about yourself. He'd love to connect with you more, but he struggles with vulnerability.

As a result of mind reading, you never get to the root of the issue. You miss opportunities to connect authentically, and problems that could be solved continue to fester.

Projection

Sometimes we're afraid to face what we feel, so we project those feelings onto other people. When you project onto someone, you attribute your feelings or thoughts onto them. For instance, you might accuse your spouse of being irritated or bored with you when, in fact, you're the one who is irritated or bored! Or he might accuse you of flirting with another man when the truth is he's struggling with a romantic attraction to another woman. Maybe you tell yourself that your friend isn't treating you well when the truth is you are harboring envy.

When you project your feelings onto others, it complicates an already complicated situation. Instead of naming what's hard inside of you and taking responsibility for your own feelings, you misname someone else's feelings, creating a barrier to relational health.

Personalization

As the name implies, this barrier involves taking things personally or assigning blame to yourself without any logical reason or evidence that you are to blame. For example, you're hosting a gathering of friends, and your sister, who is also there, seems quiet and aloof. You take her behavior personally, assuming that her aloofness is evidence that your party is a failure. The truth is the party was amazing. Your sister was simply having a bad day about something completely unrelated. Or your spouse asks you if you'd please remember to put the cap on the toothpaste tube you both share. You take it personally and assume he thinks you're inconsiderate and rude. Actually, he thinks you're wonderful! He simply prefers to have the cap on the toothpaste.

If you tend to take things personally in a relationship, it can be challenging to have practical or meaningful conversations. Instead of having a discussion with your sister about why she was so quiet, you beat yourself up for not throwing a better party. Or you lash out when your husband asks you to put the cap on the toothpaste: "Stop criticizing me!" He feels confused, and now you're in conflict.

Greener Grass

One of the most common barriers to health in relationships is what is often called "the grass is greener" syndrome. It goes something like this: *I need someone more _____.*

I need someone more affirming.

I need someone more fun.

I need someone more responsible.

When left unchecked, this syndrome creates a barrier to cherishing the good qualities that your loved one does have. Here's the thing: maybe you do need more affirmation, more fun, or more help. It doesn't work to try to gaslight yourself out of craving this quality. What's also true is that no one human has all the wonderful qualities! If you trade someone who is disciplined for someone who is a lot of fun, you're soon going to start wishing for the discipline. If you trade someone fun-loving and spontaneous for someone disciplined, you're soon going to miss the fun.

Relationships are challenging, because the humans engaging in them are complex. But those challenges are also part of the joy and adventure—and even the fun! With care and intention, you can name, frame, and brave your way through complicated feelings and into a network of vital, life-giving relationships.

Naming and Framing Complicated Feelings

Navigating mixed feelings—especially about people we feel like we *should* love—is tricky. It's as if you're navigating a path with a ditch on each side. On one side of the path is the ditch of martyrdom, where you deny what you really feel or guilt-message yourself to death. On the other side of the path is the ditch of entitlement, where you demand certain treatment or try to get the other person to fix what you don't like. Both ditches lead to bitterness and resentment.

The trick to staying on the clear path ahead of you is to name what's hard honestly while simultaneously honoring the good that you see. Here's how it works.

Start by naming what's hard inside of you. *Name what's hard. Start with yourself.*

Here are some examples:

- *I hate that she's at my house all the time!*
- *I feel anxious when he shuts me out.*
- *It really hurt that she undermined my event.*
- *I feel alone when she works all the time.*
- *I wish he were more fun.*

Don't rush to try to analyze, guilt-message, or fix the way you feel. Instead, give yourself some time to simply feel it. Linger there a moment. Take a walk or sit and notice for a spell. You're not judging the other person. You're not being cruel. It's not really even about the other person at this point. You're simply attuning to what's happening inside you.

You care about this other person *and* sometimes they annoy you! Sometimes they hurt you! Sometimes they drive you nuts. Paradoxically, when you give yourself permission to honor what's hard about a relationship, it reduces tension inside. You quiet the noise of dissonance and guilt messages. You're simply aware of what's true: *This situation is hard. I have a lot of feelings about it.*

As you move down this naming path, you're slowly entering into a place in between where you're reflecting more deeply on this situation—you're starting the work of framing. You need something, maybe from this other person, from God, from yourself, or from someone else. You might gently start asking yourself, *What do I need in this moment? What is a longing of my heart?*

Here are some examples:

- *I need more space for myself. I need more time alone.*
- *I need to feel like I'm doing all I can.*
- *I need her to know how I feel.*
- *I need more help. I need more attention. I need to feel like I'm valued and cherished.*
- *I need more fun and laughter. I long for more adventure.*

Those needs and longings make sense. It's okay to want them. You don't have to fix it yet. You don't have to figure out how to make it happen. Instead, just linger here for a little while. Notice what it's like to be present to a longing. You might invite God into the different things you're noticing. *God, I long for more of this. I don't know how to make it happen.*

As you name and frame, your mind clears a bit. You take a deep breath. You might cry or vent your frustrations. You're not alone. You're present to yourself and aware of God's Spirit. You're in that place where God always meets his children, that place of simple, childlike awareness. *I'm not okay. I need your help. I don't want to hurt this other person. I also need to figure out how to honor myself.* You're creating more spaciousness inside.

And when you're ready, after the tears or the anger or the honest self-reflection—after your body feels a little less tense—you might begin to think back on the situation that has caused you this distress. You've unlocked your complicated feelings. They're out in front of you now, where you can reflect on them, instead of trapped inside your body. You're not going to deny them anymore. You regain access to what's also true about the other person. You start laying out all the different truth-pieces.

- *I love her devotion, even when she drives me crazy.*
- *I cherish his private nature. It's so hard to parent.*
- *I love her free spirit. It also hurts me at times.*
- *I respect her work ethic, even when it's hard for me.*
- *I'm grateful for his loyalty, even though I long for more adventure.*

And you create a bigger frame, a holy reframe that accounts for all the different pieces. Here's what that might look like:

Two Things Can Be True

I LOVE	I NEED
her devotion to our family.	more space.
his private nature.	to tell him that I'm worried.
her exuberance.	to set some boundaries with it.
his work ethic.	more of his attention.
his loyalty.	more adventure.
their_____.	more_____.

As you name and frame complex truths, you quiet the noise inside your mind. You honor all the truth-pieces. You show respect and compassion for others *and* for yourself. You're able to see more clearly the possibilities ahead of you. The work of naming and framing your complicated emotions kick-starts the creativity you'll need to brave your next steps.

REFRAMING A RELATIONSHIP

Sometimes you'll need to reframe unrealistic or outdated expectations of another person. For example, perhaps a close friend isn't as available to you anymore. Maybe you no longer live in the same city. Maybe she's had children, gotten married, or become more involved in her career. Regardless, this person isn't investing in your relationship in the way you wish they would. It hurts to face this reality. But it also frees you to name it. Then create a holy reframe. *I love this person*, and *I need to release my expectations of them at this time.* Your brave step is to accept reality and stop fighting for something that simply is not there.

In other cases, you might be the one who needs to bravely empower someone else to reframe their expectations of you. Maybe you notice that a friend or family member has expectations of you that don't match what you have to give. Name and frame that honestly: *I don't want to hurt this person*, and *it's not kind to mislead them.* You might start saying "No, thank you" to invitations or requests. Or you might directly let them know that you care about them but you need to focus on other areas of your life at this time.

Braving the Crossroads with Your Loved One

It's brave to enter into the Crossroads with your loved one. It's brave to leave behind your own behaviors that create barriers to healthy communication. It's brave to fight for change, to say, "I care enough about this relationship that I want to name what's hard in it." It's also brave to decide you're going to suffer it wisely at this time; instead of speaking up, you're going to stay attentive to your own emotions, trusting the timing and the process.

Here are some examples of each of these braving options.

Leaving It Behind

You first might brave the work of leaving behind old ways of relating that don't serve you anymore. For example, you might leave behind mind reading or taking things personally. Instead, practice the skill of what I like to call "just ask." For example, you might practice saying any of the following:

- "I noticed you were quiet the other evening. Was anything wrong?"
- "Mom, I'm curious. You're spending a lot of time here. Are you doing that for you, or are you doing that for us?"
- "Honey, I'd love to understand what you were thinking when you said that. It landed kind of funny on me. I want to be sure I understand what you meant."

You can also use "just ask" when it comes to asking for support. Instead of silencing your need because you're fearful of burdening someone else, just ask. "I'm struggling today. Are you available to talk?" The other person might be available. If they're not, you can ask someone else. Either way, you're setting a powerful norm, empowering both yourself and your loved one to ask for help and state limits honestly.

If it's tempting for you to project your feelings onto others, you might leave that behind too. Instead, practice identifying your own feelings with a person who has proven safe for you. Here are some examples of how to own your own feelings:

- "I want to be present for you, and I'm also a little bit distracted right now."

- "I'm so happy for you, and I'm also honestly a little jealous!"
- "What you shared stirred up complicated emotions inside me. I want to be here for you, and I'm also noticing that I'm having my own reaction to it."

You're not hijacking the conversation, nor are you bypassing yourself. You're honoring the other person's experience while simultaneously honoring your own.

You can also leave behind the tendency to long for "greener grass." Instead of resenting your loved one for strengths they do not have, honor the good qualities they do have *and* work to get your own needs met in healthy ways. For example, if your spouse is more hardworking than he is fun, identify a girlfriend who can scratch your itch for fun. Or if your best friend isn't very affirming, seek out a mentor or another friend who gives you that nourishment. The beauty of our design is that we don't have to get all our needs met by only one person.

One of my favorite braving strategies is to develop what I call the "Rolodex approach," which means creating a robust network of people you can contact for different needs. Research suggests that we need three to five close friends and a dozen or more trusted connections in our lives.[1] By identifying several sources of support, you can adjust the expectations you have for one single person and enjoy the richness of diverse perspectives and attributes of different kinds of people.

Suffering It Wisely

Sometimes you choose to brave what I call "sitting on your wisdom" and wait to initiate a change in your relationship. Maybe you want to give the situation more time. You might want to get yourself into a better place emotionally. You're going to speak up, but you first need to increase your own support so you can speak up in a healthy way. Or you might choose to wait until the other person is in a better place emotionally. Maybe they're struggling with a stressor or a loss that's inhibiting their capacity.

What's important is that you do not bypass what you feel. Two things can be true. You can give this person space *and* honor the reality that you are making a sacrifice for the relationship. It's also important to identify a time period after which you'll reassess. Here are some examples of promises you might make to yourself to build trust while you wait:

- *I'm not going to speak up now. But if [specify the behavior] happens again, I will.* Write a script so that you are prepared.
- *I'm not going to say anything now. But I will set a boundary the next time we get together.* Define the boundary you will set for yourself.
- *I'm going to ask a trusted third party how they would view this situation. I will make my decision after that conversation.* Schedule the appointment with your trusted adviser.

NAME, FRAME, AND BRAVE CONFLICT

Most of us are adept at conflict avoidance.[2] It's one thing to decide to wait to bring up a challenging topic when the timing is right or when we feel prepared. It's another to sidestep the issue out of fear. The former is about exercising strategic patience, while the latter is driven by avoidance. When you're tempted to avoid conflict, name, frame, and brave your way to clear action steps.

Name: What is a challenging topic you need to address with your loved one?

Frame: Ask yourself the following framing questions:

- *Why am I fearful about raising the issue? Am I afraid of damaging a relationship? Facing criticism? Not being able to articulate my thoughts effectively?*
- *What strategies have I used in the past to handle conflict? How effective were they?*
- *What is the worst that could happen if I raise the topic, and how likely is it?*
- *What positive outcomes could arise from addressing the conflict?*

Brave: Identify a braving step based on your answers.

- Seek help drafting a script. Role-play with a trusted adviser.
- Practice techniques to stay calm, such as deep breathing or guided imagery.
- Identify a way to honor yourself after the conversation. No matter the outcome, celebrate that you took a brave step!

Fighting for Change

When you fight for change, you initiate a conversation with the other person. Use your "two things can be true" statements to anchor you, and select an appropriate time to speak up. It's also helpful to name your intention up front as clearly as possible. Here are some examples of how you can set yourself up well for a successful conversation:

- "No one did anything wrong, **and** we need to talk about _____. Is now a good time for you?"
- "I love seeing you, **and** I'm needing to be more intentional with my time. Are you open to a discussion about our schedules?"
- "I trust that you didn't intend to hurt me, **and** that statement hurt me. I need you to know this, because I care about our relationship."

When you lead with positivity, it creates a sense of closeness rather than conflict: "I love you! Will you join me at the Crossroads so that we can brave a healthier path together?"

BRAVING A HEALTHY CONVERSATION

If you decide to brave a conversation, it's wise to think through practical questions like these:

- When is a good time of the day to bring it up? What is a good day of the week? For example, you might not want to raise the conversation late at night, the week of your partner's big deadline, or prior to your child's debut in the school play!

- Where is the best place to have the conversation? Is it better to keep it casual (often the case with kids and teens)? Or is it better to identify a quiet space where you can both give the conversation your full attention?
- What is your primary intention? Is it shared under-standing? Is it a change in certain behaviors? Clearly naming your goal paves the way for connection.

Sometimes you'll engage in all that naming and framing work for what turns out to be a thirty second conversation. But those thirty seconds can have a tremendous impact on your own inner peace and on the relationship. For example, you might be driving with your teenage son in the car. The time feels right, and you are prepared. So you bravely wade into naming your observation: "Honey, I don't want to pry, but I've been worried about you. You don't seem like your normally happy self. Is there anything you want to talk about?" Maybe he responds. Maybe he shuts you down. Here's the thing: no matter how your child responds in this instance, you've achieved an incredibly important goal. You've let him know that you're aware and that you care. And that brave step travels miles in his heart and soul.

All that prep work might also lead to a change in *your* behavior. Maybe you're at dinner with a spouse who typically does not ask you about your day. You seize a moment of quiet to say, "I'd love to share with you something I've been thinking about." Then see how it goes. Maybe he'll recognize your bid for connection and respond to it.[3] If he does, you've just established a new avenue of connecting. If he doesn't, you can then bravely name what happened. "That was a bid for connection. I want to share with you something that matters to me. Are you open to hearing about it?" If he gets defensive or shuts down, it'll hurt, but you'll also have valuable information. You might need to brave couples' counseling or a couples' workshop focused on improving your connection.

Changing her behavior was exactly what my client Isabella decided to do as she braved the work of creating order out of the chaos in her family. Her braving steps initially focused on giving herself permission to reduce others' expectations and take charge of her own schedule. First, she scheduled time for herself. She wanted to take a walk each day by herself with her phone off. So we scheduled that time into her calendar. From there we turned to her kids. She scheduled weekly one-on-one time alone with her daughter and a bedtime routine that allowed her quality time with each of her children. Next Isabella blocked off a weekly family dinner with her dad, as well as time to take a weekly walk with her sister. As she looked over her new calendar, she saw order and harmony. She could maximize the quality of time she spent with each person without getting overwhelmed. Then she began to enforce her new schedule. "I love you, Dad, and we want you to come over every Friday evening to hang out with us. If you need me during the week, I need you to call first." "Kids, I won't be available during this window of time each day. If you need something, you'll need to call your dad or your aunt." With the order of a schedule in front of her, she began to find her voice.

Weaving Together a New Story

The best, healthiest relationships are strong enough and flexible enough to honor the whole story of all your experiences together—the moments of hurt *and* the moments of sweet harmony. The moments of awkward miscommunication *and* the moments of glorious connection.

> **THE BEST, HEALTHIEST RELATIONSHIPS ARE STRONG ENOUGH AND FLEXIBLE ENOUGH TO HONOR THE WHOLE STORY OF ALL YOUR EXPERIENCES TOGETHER.**

As you name, frame, and brave complexity within your relationships, each truth-piece becomes a treasured part of the larger story. It's as if you're creating a giant quilt that tells the whole story of your relationship. Some patches of the quilt almost ripped apart. You can see where you had to mend the tear, but you love that section now—the work you did held up for the long haul. Another section of the quilt is faded—a reminder that you drifted apart for a season. You almost lost each other, but that wasn't the end of your story.

And then you see those vibrant patches. The ones where the colors are vivid and clear. They might represent the good times. Or they might represent the awkward conversations and the miscommunications that you can now laugh about with each other. You look at all the material you have yet to work with—there's so much left to weave together. You're not sure exactly what it will look like, but you're confident. You know how to face what's hard. And deep inside you know that nothing could tear this tapestry apart—this rich story of your relationship that you've worked so hard to create together.

ELEVEN

I Shouldn't Feel Conflicted About God

Katie was on the verge of sabotaging her faith. She just didn't know it. In the face of a million competing emotions, she was trying to force-fit a spiritual solution that did not account for all of them. She was stuck neck-deep in her conflicting thoughts and feelings. Instead of facing them, she was projecting a major decision onto God.

"How are you today?" Katie asked warmly the first time we met. "What a great couch. Where did you find it?" she continued, as if we were neighbors casually chatting rather than client and therapist starting our first appointment.

"I'm well, Katie. Thank you for asking."

"And your family? Is everyone well?" she continued pleasantly.

"Yes, we are all well," I replied.

Conflicting feelings began to surface inside me. *Should I continue with the pleasantries? Or should I play the therapist trump card?*

"I'd love to hear more about what brings you here to see me, Katie."

Katie folded her hands in her lap, carefully adjusted her blouse, and looked at me warmly. "I'm about to get married for the first time," she said politely, "but I don't love him."

"You don't love him?"

"No, I don't love him. I believe God is calling me to marry him. But if it were up to me, I wouldn't."

And then she crumbled into tears.

"Why would God do this to me?" she sobbed.

It was all I could do to keep a neutral expression on my face. But the truth is I had heard a version of this story countless times before, though perhaps not as extreme. *God wants me to do the thing I hate the most. I just have to do it God's way. This is the cross I have to bear.*

Underneath such rationalizations is often unnamed fear, doubt, or uncertainty. The dissonance festers, but instead of working our way through it, we pretend like we have it all together. On the inside we battle. But we tell ourselves *I shouldn't feel this way—especially about God!*

The Problem with Spiritual Bypassing

If you grew up in a faith community, you may have been taught to spiritually bypass the complex feelings you experience. Spiritual bypassing is essentially a thinking trap. It ignores the richness and complexity of your God-given design. You feel confused, scared, or uncertain. You don't know what to think or do. Instead of carefully working through the different layers of a complicated problem, you try to force-fit a spiritual pseudo solution. For example, you might tell yourself things like the following:

- *All I need is prayer!*
- *Forgive and forget. That's the best way to approach this situation.*
- *Let go and let God.*

Sometimes you spiritually bypass yourself. When you're conflicted inside, it's tempting to default to a subtle form of overspiritualizing—*God would want me to do it!* Or *It must be God's will!* Or *It's the Christian thing to do!* But does God *really* want you to do it? Is it *really* God's will? Is it *really* the Christian thing to do? Instead of engaging your mind and the tools God has given you, in addition to your spiritual resources, you project your decision-making onto God. You give God too much responsibility for the decisions that you, in fact, are making. It's the ultimate counterfeit trump card against inner conflict: *I can't figure out what to do, so I'll use God as a scapegoat.*

Oftentimes other people encourage you to spiritually bypass—they assume that all your problems can be solved with a spiritual solution. A friend might encourage you to jump to forgiveness when what's really needed is to grieve a betrayal and establish healthy boundaries. Or a faith community might encourage you to spiritualize a problem that is not primarily spiritual. For example, a spiritual leader might encourage you to pray harder for God to take away your depression or medical condition instead of helping you to find a professional who is trained to help you. Or they might encourage you to love the person harming you instead of helping you to protect yourself.

Spiritual bypassing keeps you from adequately addressing the problem you are facing. It also creates dissonance inside, or internal discomfort. You want to trust in God, but the problem is only getting worse. You start to blame yourself: *If only my faith were stronger!* As a result of that inner tension, you resort to any of the following unhealthy coping strategies:

- **Self-gaslighting:** telling yourself you don't feel what you really feel
- **Numbing:** suppressing your emotions instead of working to cope with them
- **Magical thinking:** disregarding reality and denying yourself the opportunity to discover practical solutions

You miss out on opportunities to develop skills, gain knowledge, or receive care and comfort from others.

Here's what is true: God created you with an ensemble of interconnected parts, including thoughts, emotions, and a nervous system, designed to work together harmoniously like an orchestra. Your job, in partnership with God's Spirit, is to be the conductor of that orchestra, working patiently with all the pieces, bringing them out of dissonance and into a cohesive melody.

And that's exactly the kind of work that my client Katie needed to do. Instead of facing her complicated feelings and working her way through them, she had tried to drown them out: *It's God's will that I marry him!* But parts of Katie weren't sure about this decision. Parts of her were scared and anxious. Katie needed to patiently work through each of the truth-pieces in partnership with God until she arrived at a cadence that accounted for all the parts of her story.

Katie's case was indeed complicated. I'll admit that at first I assumed she and her fiancé weren't a good match. I was concerned about her apparent lack of feelings for Ike, the man to whom she was engaged. But as I set aside my own conflicting thoughts and assumptions and helped Katie painstakingly examine the many truth-pieces of her situation, a different picture emerged for both of us.

Katie had grown up with a significant amount of trauma, including having been abused by her father at a very young age. As a result, she had often been drawn to men who discarded or mistreated her. Toxic dynamics felt familiar to her, and she mistook familiarity for safety.

But Ike was different. He was kind, patient, and loving. He treated Katie with respect. He wasn't flashy, nor did he sweep her off her feet. The safety she experienced with him confused her—she didn't recognize it as the buzzy chemicals she had often mistaken for love. As we worked together, it became clear that she loved Ike deeply and recognized that he was a man who would be a true, loving companion through all the seasons of her life. A part of her, however, didn't recognize her feelings for Ike as love. This part of her experienced the safety she found in Ike as boring or uneventful— unlike the dramatic highs and lows of prior relationships. She was drawn to Ike, but she was also confused. Instead of working her way through the conflict inside, she had tried to force-fit a spiritual solution: *God wants me to do it!* In some ways this conclusion wasn't unwise. But it also wasn't fair to herself, God, or Ike.

The truth was that the confused part of Katie needed her care and attention. She didn't need to bypass her mixed feelings. She needed to name, frame, and brave a deeper understanding of herself and of her relationship to Ike. She needed more time to completely fill out the missing pieces of this puzzle.

GOD DOESN'T ASK YOU TO BYPASS THE CONFLICTING EMOTIONS YOU FACE.

God doesn't ask you to bypass the conflicting emotions you face. What if those feelings are an opportunity to brave even deeper growth and healing?

Naming Spiritual Complexity

It's normal to experience confusion, doubt, anger, fear, or disappointment when it comes to God. You could even argue that Jesus experienced complicated feelings toward God. As he anguished in the garden of Gethsemane, you can almost sense the desperation in his prayer. *Really, God? Really? I've got to go through this?*

A relationship with God is like any relationship—it involves complicated feelings. *I want to pray, but I am so angry! I want to believe God is good, but I see so much suffering. I want to trust God with this decision, but I'm not certain.*

You might also experience complicated feelings about yourself in relationship to God. *I can't turn to God right now; I'm too far gone.*

I've done such terrible things; how could God love me? I should trust God, but frankly, I'd rather trust myself today!

Walking by faith is a delicate tightrope. It's the ultimate both/and. It involves trusting God *and* honoring the way you really feel.

You can have faith *and* feel scared, confused, or uncertain.

You can trust God *and* experience anger, disappointment, or doubt.

You can follow Jesus *and* be uncertain how to apply his teachings.

I would argue that true faith is the work of constantly reconciling what's impossibly hard with a hope in what's unfathomably good and beautiful. If you overweight either one, you miss out on the fullness of an active, dynamic relationship.

If you are someone who chafes against naive spiritual platitudes or who wrestles with complicated feelings about God or faith, you're in good company. This wrestling *is* the work of faith.

The good news is that, as with any relationship, when you name your complicated feelings, you invest in a deeper, more authentic bond. Instead of bypassing them, start naming them *with* God.

We often try to shove these feelings aside and manipulate ourselves into feeling what we "should" feel. Or we process these feelings with friends or loved ones without ever processing them with God. But what if spiritual maturity is bringing all of what you feel—including your anger, doubt, and confusion—into your relationship with God?

No matter where you are, whether you're journaling, waiting in the car pickup lane, or grocery shopping, simply start to name the different truth-pieces you feel and then address each one to God—a practice I like to call "Comma, God."

I'm worried becomes *I'm worried, God. I don't understand what's happening.*

I need help becomes *I need help, God. I don't know what to do.*

I'm sad becomes *I'm sad, God. I feel so alone.*

I don't want to pray becomes *I don't want to pray, God. I'm kinda mad at you right now.*

Just like that you're engaged in a prayer. You become aware of yourself in the present moment, *and* you become aware of God. Research shows that when you dwell on God and not only on yourself, you reduce stress and anxiety and increase your ability to tolerate painful experiences.[1]

To be clear, what you believe about this God with whom you're connecting matters. Is this a God who loves you? Is this a God who's for you? Is this a God who takes you by the hand and walks with you through the trials that you face? If it's not, it's wise to reconsider the messages you've internalized about God. Imagine if a child were to come running to you angry or scared. Would you rebuke her or offer her a platitude? "You really shouldn't feel that way!" "Choose joy!" Of course not. You would pull her close to you and give her the gift of your presence. "It's hard to feel angry." "I'm here with you." "I want to understand." You'd give her compassion. Tenderness. A sense that she's not alone.

Similarly, when we're mad, scared, uncertain, or heartbroken, we rarely need a reprimand or a pat answer. We need presence. We need attunement. That doesn't mean we don't also want answers. We do. But just like a hurting child, we first always need connection. That's how God made us! If we know how to soothe a child who is hurting, how much more does the one who made us know how to attune to us in our sadness, hurt, or despair?[2]

Like a tender, loving parent, God meets us with compassionate presence—in all of our complexity. God doesn't always fix things right away. But he does not ask us to bypass what we feel. He does not gaslight us. He does not ask us to pretend.

When we're hurting, God gives us the gift of honoring the truth of what we feel.

The paradox is that when you name what's hard—what's true in this very moment—you open yourself to God's with-ness.[3] You stop trying to analyze your motives or earn God's approval. You stop trying to fix yourself or figure out God. You move into the present moment. You attune to what you really feel, and God's Spirit attunes right there with you.

You're never closer to God than when you're naming what's hard. You're telling the truth, and telling the truth is God's sweet spot.

Naming and Framing Counterfeit Messages About God

When you name what's hard, you tend to bump into old messages you've outgrown, messages that keep you from growing deeper in genuine faith. You might be surprised at some of the messages you've picked up that interfere with an honest, authentic relationship with God. Counterfeit, simplistic versions of otherwise beautifully rich spiritual concepts—such as what it means to love others, show faithfulness, experience joy, confess sin, or forgive—are rampant. These messages linger in your mind, often outside your conscious awareness, creating dissonance inside.

Naming those messages helps you tame them. You can then determine where you picked them up and why you've believed them so that you can develop a truer viewpoint instead. Here are some of the most common counterfeit messages I observe in my work with clients and some ways to reframe them.

I should feel happy in my suffering. Passages like James 1:2 can be taken out of context and misinterpreted as suggesting that you should always feel happy. This counterfeit message encourages a false version of joy. The truth is that joy is a complex emotion intimately linked with experiences of sadness, grief, and pain.

If I had more faith, I wouldn't be struggling. Some religious circles equate faith in God with health, financial success, or happiness. This counterfeit message pressures you to project an image of being "blessed" or successful as evidence of your faith. The truth is that faith is no guarantee against suffering. Instead, God promises that as you persevere through suffering, you'll develop character and hope.[4]

I should just die to myself. Jesus' teaching about self-denial can be misconstrued to suggest that you should never consider your own needs—a misapplication contrary to how Jesus lived his own life. This counterfeit message promotes a false version of sacrifice, encouraging you to disregard toxicity or boundary violations instead of working to protect and care for yourself. The truth is that sacrifice is a delicate balance of selflessness and self-respect.

I should always feel content. While contentment is a virtue, it's a cultivated skill, not a quick fix. This counterfeit message promotes a false version of peace, encouraging you to bypass negative feelings. The truth is that acknowledging frustrations or areas of discontent can help you grow and change aspects of your life, yielding more contentment.

I should forgive and forget. Forgiveness is a central tenet of Jesus' teaching, and it's an incredibly nuanced concept. The counterfeit version of forgiveness encourages you to minimize or overlook legitimate wrongs. The truth is that acknowledging hurt and injustice is critical to ensuring that resentment and bitterness don't fester in your soul—the primary goal of forgiveness.

I'm a terrible sinner! The term *sin* reflects a complex theological belief about the imperfect nature of humans and the need for redemption through Christ. The counterfeit version of confessing sin induces shame, false guilt, or control. On the other hand, when you name the imperfections you see in yourself honestly in a loving environment, you find freedom, acceptance, and belonging—the opposite of shame.

You don't have to dupe yourself into counterfeit versions of faith, hope, love, forgiveness, peace, or joy. Our God is so much deeper and richer and more intricate than the simplistic formulas we're so often given. Be honest about what you feel and create a place in between to reflect on the different truth-pieces in partnership with God's Spirit.

SPIRITUAL FRAMING QUESTIONS

- **Facts:** *What counterfeit messages have I believed?*
- **Roots:** *Where did I pick up these messages? When did I start to believe them?*

- **Audit:** *Are these messages true? Do they yield spiritual fruit (love, joy, peace, patience, kindness, goodness, faithfulness, gentleness, or self-control[5]) in my life?*
- **Mental Messages:** *What messages do I tell myself about how God views me? What messages do I tell myself about how God wants me to treat others?*
- **Expansion:** *What do different passages from the Bible say about these messages? What are some different ways of interpreting those passages?*

This type of framing is exactly what I did in my work with Katie: "Do you believe God wants you to marry someone you don't love? Is that true? Where did you pick that message up?" Katie began to unpack different messages about God's love, an endeavor that took her right back to her childhood trauma. Instead of protecting her, her dad had blamed Katie for his abusive actions. She didn't understand what a good father's love felt like. She was confused about God, and she was confused about Ike.

Framing the messages she'd internalized about love helped Katie grow in understanding herself and her past wounds. She became more honest about the paradoxes she held inside.

I want to trust that God has good gifts for me, and *I don't always trust that God does.*

I want to receive Ike's love, and *I'm terrified to trust Ike.*

I'm all in with this relationship, and *I need more time.*

As Katie patiently gained a deeper understanding of her complicated feelings about God and love, she also gained clarity. She realized she loved and cherished Ike. She believed he was a good gift from a good God who loved her. She wanted to build a life with Ike. She also needed more time to heal from her past so that when she did commit to Ike, every part of her could celebrate. Her next brave step wasn't to plan a wedding—that would come in time. First, she needed to brave deeper intimacy, to share with Ike about the impact of her childhood trauma.

So much of authentic faith is leaning into the paradox that two things really are so very often true.

I trust you, God, and *I'm scared.*

I want to forgive, and *I need to protect myself.*

I'm grieving, and *I'm also healing.*

My anger is valid, and *I'm responsible for regulating it.*

I feel less than, and *I'm learning to see myself as God does.*

I miss the mark, and *I'm fearfully and wonderfully made.*

Honoring the complexity of faith is also deeply biblical:

"I do believe; help me overcome my unbelief!"—the father of a boy possessed by a spirit.[6]

"Take this cup from me. Yet not what I will, but what you will."—Jesus.[7]

"Though he slay me, yet will I hope in him."—Job.[8]

"Why, my soul, are you downcast? . . . I will yet praise him, my Savior and my God."—David.[9]

It takes work to name and frame old messages and brave a more whole, more resilient, sturdier faith. But the good news is that as you align yourself with all of what's true, you start working with the

I SHOULDN'T FEEL THIS WAY

grain of God's universe, including the grain of the universe God has placed inside of you.[10]

Braving Holistic Spiritual Practices

The antidote to spiritual bypassing is to brave a holistic relationship with God, one that includes all of your being, including the complexity of your thoughts and emotions.[11] You're fighting for a more vital relationship with God and working out your salvation—your wholeness—with all of your heart, soul, and strength.[12] You might need to bravely leave old messages, old shame, or even old practices behind. You also might have to suffer some questions or doubts wisely. Here are some examples of braving steps you might take.

Whole Body Prayer

Many of us have the idea that praying means sitting quietly with our heads bowed and eyes closed. We measure the success of our prayers by the intensity of emotion or the minutes on the clock. But what if you incorporated your whole being into your prayer, including your thoughts, feelings, and even your body?

For example, in chapter 5 you learned how to mind your mind throughout your day—to pay attention to your thoughts. As you mind your mind while cooking or gardening or walking or driving to work, consider inviting God into the process of attuning to your thoughts.

I'm worried about my child, my health, my bills. Help me to think clearly about what's really going on, God. Be with me as I work to get to the root of my fear.

I can't shake this idea that someone is mad at me. Help me to consider the facts of the situation, God. Guide me to discern if I did something wrong or if this is false guilt.

I'm wrestling with anger. I'm frustrated that this person is getting away with harmful behavior, God. I'm not willing to be harmed anymore. Lead my thoughts as I consider how to protect myself.

Likewise, in chapter 6 you identified different activities to help you process negative emotions instead of numbing. You might incorporate conversations with God into the recreational, sensory, or physical activities you identified. For example, when you become aware of painful emotions, consider walking outside, eyes wide open, and naming what you notice as an act of praise.

I see that mountain, God. It reminds me of your strength.

That tree is beautiful, God. It reminds me that all seasons pass.

I'm grateful for the sun that always rises, God. It reminds me of your constancy.

Finally, in chapter 7 you learned how to ground yourself when your nervous system is activated—when you're experiencing an intense reaction in your body. When a child is scared or upset, you'd first gently soothe him by pulling him close and taking deep breaths. As he's soothed, he's more able to communicate with you about what happened. Similarly, when you're activated, it can be hard to pray in the way most of us have been taught. It's helpful to calm your nervous system as you articulate what you feel or what you need. Consider the difference between the following prayers.

God, I'm desperate. Please make this go away. I can't take this anymore!

As you pray, your heart is racing, your body is tense. You're begging God to intervene in your situation. Now compare that to this prayer.

God, I'm struggling (deep breath).

I know you're with me (deep breath).

I'm scared (deep breath).

I need you (deep breath).

God designed your body to release endorphins and good chemicals when you breathe, sing, experience nature, or move. Incorporating any of these activities as you name what's hard with God helps you soothe your nervous system.

Braving Healing Communities

Sometimes you'll brave an entirely new faith community. The first time I experienced the pain and dissonance that come as a result of church-sanctioned spiritual bypassing was while I was working at a Christian summer camp as a college student. During an early Bible study, a leader of the camp taught us that if we didn't hear the voice of Jesus whispering in our ear, telling us what to do each day, there was something wrong with our faith.

I didn't hear the voice of Jesus that summer, at least not in the way the Bible teacher thought I should. Instead, I watched as my peers sought to showcase the superiority of their spirituality through quoting Bible passages and public displays of morality. All the while, not one word was said about the cliques, overt racism, and cruel jokes about the very people we were there to serve that permeated staff culture.

The dissonance inside me that summer was almost intolerable.

I felt heartsick and confused. Not about Jesus—I knew that the hypocrisy I witnessed was not the fruit of listening to his voice. Still, I was confused about how people who claimed to follow Jesus could be so horrible to other people. Somehow, even at that young age, I knew it was okay to feel what I felt. I named it and framed it constantly with God. *How could people who claim to love you and hear your voice behave in these ways?* I didn't force myself to pretend it was okay.

Over time, this relentless naming and framing paid off—I began to see how I could brave a healing path. I couldn't change that experience. But I could do my part to help others who were hurt by toxic spiritual cultures. I braved the work of becoming a therapist, where I could help bring healing to others who experienced the pain of church hurt and spiritual trauma.

Over time, my family and I also braved a whole different kind of church community, one where the focus was on caring for those who were hurting the most, those suffering tremendous pain, addictions, homelessness, and debilitating mental illnesses. In that community we felt connected and accepted in ways we'd never felt before.

One of the practices we came to cherish was a time each Sunday during the service to give testimony. I was always amazed by the honest naming that ensued.

"I'm Bob, and I didn't use last night, even though I really wanted to."

We love you, Bob!

"I'm Peggy. I found a wallet, and I really wanted to steal the money in it. But I didn't!"

We love you, Peggy!

"I'm Stan. I'm depressed, but I got out of bed this morning. Praise be to God!"

We love you, Stan!

And I began to brave a new vision for what it means to be in community. What if we all learned to name together honestly? What if we lovingly attuned to each other's struggles instead of fixing them? What if we could chase away old messages of shame and counterfeit virtues?

"I'm Matt, and my heart is broken today."

We love you, Matt!

"I'm Ann, and I cannot stop people-pleasing."

Welcome, Ann!

"I'm Joanie, and I'm so mad at my friend."

Good to see you, Joanie!

"I'm Chad, and I relapsed last night."

Welcome, Chad!

"I'm Sue, and I yelled at my kids this morning."

Me too! We're so glad you're here.

As we name together without shame, we become a truer, more beautiful oasis—an embodied experience of Christ—for each other. Psychiatrist and fellow therapist Curt Thompson wrote in his beautiful book *The Soul of Desire* about small groups of people he leads called "confessional communities." In these communities, individuals gather to name their longings, heartbreaks, and traumas—what Curt said are "all acts of prayer," creating spaces for connection and transformation.[13] As Curt wrote so powerfully:

It is in communities like these that we encounter the possibility of being deeply known and where we practice for heaven. It is in a body of like-minded people who are working hard to tell their stories as truly as they can that Jesus shows up, right in the middle of their narratives . . . and utters, in the voices of others in the room, "Peace be with you!"[14]

I experience what Curt described, not only within my church community but also with my sister and two childhood friends. We gather regularly with the purpose to name, frame, and brave what's hard in our lives. As one person shares the truth-pieces of a fragmented story, the others listen attentively—not to solve the problem but to bear witness to all the pieces. As a result of being attuned to in this way, we each catch glimpses of a truer, more beautiful picture of our lives.

In safe contexts like these, we can also brave naming our own sin. We can name our shortcomings. We can name our secrets, without fear of shame entering in.

"I lashed out."

"I reached for the booze."

"I lied."

Yes. This is true.

Here's what's also true: You are worthy. You are forgiven. You are loved.

As a result of being seen and known by a loving community, we grow stronger and steadier, surer of ourselves, our convictions, and our purpose. We develop a deeper sense of integrity within ourselves, with others, and with the one who made us.

A Deeper Faith

If you've been taught that working out your faith should be simple, unthinking, or one-size-fits-all, I would argue that you've been taught wrong. The Bible is not a simple book. Following Jesus is not always straightforward. Learning how to forgive, walk by faith, love others, and live joyfully takes skill. It requires you to attend to various truth-pieces and, in partnership with God's Spirit, name, frame, and brave your way through complexity. Shallow, simplistic formulas won't cut it. Not in this world. Not when Jesus lived.

The good news is that, like your Maker, you are beautifully vast and rich and wonderfully deep and intricate. You were made with the capacity to attune to your inner being—to shape the content and direction of your own thoughts and emotions and even the responses of your nervous system. Learning to access and harness the power of your God-made design to shape your life is one of the most joyful and lasting sources of satisfaction.

As a tree grows tall and strong over time, its root system spreads out, providing more stability to the tree and tapping into a broader range of nutrients. The complexity of the root system contributes to the overall strength and resilience of the tree. The same is true with your spiritual growth. When you do the work to navigate uncertainty, process disappointments, and grieve painful experiences with God, you become stronger, wiser, more resilient, even as you expand to tap into a broader range of spiritual practices.

YOU DON'T HAVE TO CHOOSE BETWEEN HONORING YOURSELF AND HONORING THE GOD WHO MADE YOU.

You don't have to choose between honoring yourself and honoring the God who made you. The choice is a false dichotomy. Instead, you can connect to yourself *and* to God honestly. You can name what's hard *and* claim your hope. You can honor conflicting feelings *and* honor the depth of your faith.

The Paradox of Hope

Navigating inner complexity is like learning to ride a bike.

It takes your whole body working in coordination. Your feet and legs have to pedal even as your hands and arms hold the handlebars steady. The core of your body works to keep you balanced. Your eyes scan the road ahead of you. It's tricky to learn at first. You practice and practice and practice, and suddenly you're doing it! The person who was trailing along behind you has let go, and you're mastering this instrument called your life.

You're wobbly, yet exhilarated. Fearful, yet excited.

Aware of the obstacles, yet confident. Alert, yet calm.

You're in command. You know how to navigate this path.

You catch a glimmer of what hope feels like.

Glimmers are the opposite of triggers.[1] When you're triggered, your whole being is activated—you're tense, stressed, and stuck in negative emotions: *I shouldn't feel this way!* On the other hand, glimmers refer to those moments when your whole being is calm, clear, and steady. *I want to feel this way!*

Valued.

Fulfilled.

At peace.

Your body is at ease, and you experience positive feelings like creativity, confidence, or even playfulness. You experience what the Bible calls *hope*. Consider what the apostle Paul said about the paradox of hope:

> We also glory in our sufferings, because we know that suffering produces perseverance; perseverance, character; and character, hope. And hope does not put us to shame, because God's love has been poured out into our hearts through the Holy Spirit, who has been given to us.[2]

To experience glimmers of hope, you have to face what's hard. You have to practice the awkward motions of naming what's wrong, examining the truth-pieces, and reflecting on what's not working. Sometimes you tumble to the ground. You ask for help. You get back up. Hope emerges as you find your way *through* the suffering.[3] It's a paradox. There's no comfort if you don't face the truth of exactly where you are.

Do you remember Dorothy, the heroine of the classic film *The Wizard of Oz*? Dorothy finds herself at a Crossroads when a tornado picks her up and plunks her down in a strange new place far from the home she longs for. She's lost, uncertain, and alone. No doubt her mind is a flurry of activity when she finds herself in this new place. But she is clear about one thing: this is not her home.

Her hope for her true home does not waver. Never once does she second-guess herself or try to convince herself that her predicament is really not that bad. She doesn't numb out or simply decide Oz is good enough. She doesn't gaslight herself.

She also honors the place where she has landed.

She wants to go home, *and* she fully inhabits the place where she is. As a result, she stays attentive and alert. She accomplishes a lot in the place in between: she helps her friends, defeats a wicked witch, and confronts toxicity.

When the time is right, she is ready. She clicks her heels together and claims the deepest longing of her heart: "There's no place like home."

What is your home, the place you long for with all your heart? What is that image, that vision, that fantasy of home in your mind? Is it love? Peace? Belonging? Freedom? Health? Picture it in your mind and hold it in your heart. Find something to remind you of that home and hang it where you see it every day.

This is your *I want to feel* this *way*.

Then, like Dorothy, name what's hard, frame your reality, and bravely step out. In doing so, you *hope*. That doesn't mean you sit around feeling hopeful. That means you *hope*. You breathe. You pray. You move. You wrestle. You cry. You laugh. You take action. You *hope*.

Counterfeit hope bypasses reality. It ignores landmines and obstacles. It pretends everything is just fine, even though you're floundering. It's like offering someone a shiny, red, plastic apple when they're starved for real nourishment! True hope, on the other hand, enters into reality. It helps you name what's hard. It helps you unearth deeper understanding. And as a result, it catalyzes you into brave action. Shame is eradicated. You experience the thrill of working your way through a tangled-up mess and discovering a beautiful clearing, a whole new adventure, on the other side.

Best of all, you find hope *within* the journey. You start to activate glimmers of hope every step along the way. You activate hope when you catch yourself in a thinking trap and redirect your thoughts with patient, tender care. You activate hope when you gently nourish yourself through pain, instead of numbing. You activate hope when you patiently soothe your nervous system. You activate hope when you name toxicity for what it is. You no longer fear suffering or hardship, because you've learned how to brave it—to create harmony out of dissonance. Calm out of chaos. Peace out of pieces. The entire process—naming, framing, and braving—becomes a virtuous cycle of hope.

You're riding the bike! You're taking charge of this beautiful life you've been given. You're shattering the divide between where you are now and where you want to go. You're shattering the divide between what's hard and the goodness you long to see. You're shattering the divide between the pain of this earth and the glorious hope of heaven.

Acknowledgments

I have always loved a good framework—a way of simplifying what is inherently complex. The experience of developing the one presented in this book was exhilarating, daunting, and incredibly meta. I found myself constantly needing to rely on the very framework I was trying to piece together. It's a journey that would have been impossible without the wise, patient support of my loved ones and trusted advisers.

To my husband, Joe, I could not have created this framework without you. You showed me the power of naming and framing from our earliest conversations. Thank you for embodying this work. I am so grateful that we get to name, frame, and brave our way through this life together.

To my astute and capable agent, Rachel Jacobson, your integrity and steady guidance are gifts. To my talented editor, Jessica Rogers, thank you for your thoughtful insights and for anchoring me at key moments of this writing process. To Kathryn Duke, Kristen Golden, Claire Drake, Lisa Beech, and the entire Thomas Nelson family, thank you for bringing your invaluable expertise to this project.

To Kate Wilder, thank you for believing in me and for your helpful feedback at the earliest stages of the manuscript. To Cindy Gao, I'm grateful for your support.

To Aundi, Rebecca, Missy, Row, and Monique, thank you for being such amazing naming partners throughout this writing process. To Laura C., you stepped in with such wisdom at key moments. Thank you. To my clients, podcast listeners, and readers, I learn so much from your dedication to this work of healing and growth. You make it all worthwhile.

To my sister, Courtney, and my bonus sisters, Jenianne and Becky, you've traveled with me through my earliest memories of inner turmoil all the way to the present day. Thank you for your faithful presence. To Mom and Dad, thank you for the example you set of braving life with integrity. To Brooke and Chase, thank you for getting me up from my desk and out into nature, where clarity so often comes to light.

And to the triune God, the ultimate source of naming, thank you for inviting each one of us into your work of healing. It is only through you and your kind, loving guidance that we find our way through the haze.

Notes

Chapter 1: The Crossroads

1. George Markowsy, "Information Theory," *Britannica*, last updated December 15, 2023, https://www.britannica.com/science/information-theory.
2. Julie Tseng and Jordan Poppenk, "Brain Meta-State Transitions Demarcate Thoughts Across Task Contexts Exposing the Mental Noise of Trait Neuroticism," *Nature Communications* 11, no. 3480 (July 13, 2020), https://doi.org/10.1038/s41467-020-17255-9.
3. Debra Trampe, Jordi Quoidbach, and Maxime Taquet, "Emotions in Everyday Life," *PLoS One* 10, no. 12 (December 23, 2015), https://doi.org/10.1371/journal.pone.0145450.
4. John 8:32.
5. If you've read my book with Kimberly Miller, *Boundaries for Your Soul*, you might think of using this framework with any part of the soul that you encounter.

Chapter 2: Name What's Hard

1. For more on how naming changes the brain, see Dan Siegel, *Mindsight: The New Science of Personal Transformation* (New York: Bantam, 2010).
2. The importance of nonjudgmental awareness is part of the well-researched practice of mindfulness. Dr. Jon Kabat-Zinn is credited with popularizing mindfulness through the development of his

Mindfulness-Based Stress Reduction (MBSR) program in the late 1970s. To learn more about his approach, see *Wherever You Go, There You Are: Mindfulness Meditation in Everyday Life*, 10th ed. (New York: Hachette, 2023).

3. Dr. James Pennebaker pioneered this approach in the 1980s and conducted foundational research demonstrating its health benefits. Numerous studies support his findings; for example, see Oliver Glass et al., "Expressive Writing to Improve Resilience to Trauma: A Clinical Feasibility Trial," *Complementary Therapies in Clinical Practice* 34 (February 2019): 240–46, https://doi.org/10.1016/j.ctcp.2018.12.005.

4. Daniel J. Siegel, *Mindsight: The New Science of Personal Transformation* (New York: Bantam, 2010), 160.

5. An example of a feelings wheel can be found online at https://feelings wheel.com.

6. Alison Cook and Kimberly Miller, *Boundaries for Your Soul: How to Turn Your Overwhelming Thoughts and Feelings into Your Greatest Allies* (Nashville: Nelson Books, 2018).

7. For a helpful overview of eighty-six emotions, see Brené Brown, *Atlas of the Heart: Mapping Meaningful Connection and the Language of Human Experience* (New York: Random House, 2021).

8. Daniel J. Siegel and Tina Payne Bryson, *The Whole-Brain Child: 12 Revolutionary Strategies to Nurture Your Child's Developing Mind* (New York: Random House, 2011), 41.

9. Siegel and Bryson, *Whole-Brain Child*, 43.

10. Richard Schwartz, founder of the Internal Family Systems model of therapy, identified the eight *C*'s as a way of describing the qualities of the Self, what my coauthor Kimberly Miller and I call the "Spirit-led Self." For more on the eight *C*'s, see Richard C. Schwartz, *Introduction to the Internal Family Systems Model* (Oak Park, IL: Trailheads Publications, 2001), 33–48.

11. Genesis 17:3–5; Matthew 1:21.

12. Exodus 32:7; 2 Samuel 12; Matthew 21:12–13.

13. C. S. Lewis, *The Screwtape Letters* (1942; repr., New York: HarperOne, 2001), 60.

Chapter 3: Frame Your Reality

1. For more on the wilderness experience of the Israelites, see Deuteronomy 1:6–8.
2. James R. Bailey and Scheherazade Rehman, "Don't Underestimate the Power of Self-Reflection," *Harvard Business Review: Ascend*, March 4, 2022, https://hbr.org/2022/03/dont-underestimate-the-power-of-self-reflection.
3. Rainer Maria Rilke, *Letters to a Young Poet* (New York: W. W. Norton, 1954), 27.
4. 1 Kings 19:12.
5. Alison Cook, *The Best of You: Break Free from Painful Patterns, Mend Your Past, and Discover Your True Self in God* (Nashville: Nelson Books, 2022), 100–104.
6. Genesis 32:22–32.

Chapter 4: Brave a New Path

1. For more on radical acceptance, see Marsha M. Linehan, *DBT Skills Training Manual*, 2nd ed. (New York: Guilford Press, 2015).
2. William R. Miller, *On Second Thought: How Ambivalence Shapes Your Life* (New York: Guilford Press, 2022), 5.
3. Miller, *On Second Thought*, 6.
4. F. Scott Fitzgerald, "The Crack-Up," *Esquire Classic*, February 1, 1936, https://classic.esquire.com/article/share/97a6b0a8-ba1c-4b7b-aa64-0d08dd9fb952; emphasis added.
5. Miller, *On Second Thought*, 20.
6. Miller, 126.
7. This chart is based on the Decisional Balance Worksheet from the Motivational Interviewing Network of Trainers, accessed January 30, 2024, PDF, https://www.motivationalinterviewing.org/sites/default/files/decisionalbalance.pdf.
8. Alison Cook, *The Best of You: Break Free from Painful Patterns, Mend Your Past, and Discover Your True Self in God* (Nashville: Nelson Books, 2022), 98.

Chapter 5: I Shouldn't Feel Stuck in My Head

1. Leon Festinger, *A Theory of Cognitive Dissonance* (Stanford, CA: Stanford University Press, 1957).
2. For more on the relationship between defensiveness and cognitive dissonance, see Azizul Halim Yahya and Vidi Sukmayadi, "A Review of Cognitive Dissonance Theory and Its Relevance to Current Social Issues," *MIMBAR: Jurnal Sosial Dan Pembangunan* 36, no. 2 (2020): 480–88, https://doi.org/10.29313/mimbar.v36i2.6652.
3. Michelle P. Maidenberg, "Beware of Your Self-Fulfilling Prophecy," *Psychology Today*, October 12, 2021, https://www.psychologytoday.com/us/blog/being-your-best-self/202110/beware-your-self-fulfilling-prophecy.
4. 2 Corinthians 10:5.
5. 1 Samuel 13:14; Acts 13:22.
6. 2 Samuel 12:7–14.

Chapter 6: I Shouldn't Feel Like Numbing My Emotions

1. For more on numbing and the many forms it takes, see Brené Brown, *Daring Greatly: How the Courage to Be Vulnerable Transforms the Way We Live, Love, Parent, and Lead* (New York: Avery, 2012).
2. Anna Lembke, *Dopamine Nation: Finding Balance in the Age of Indulgence* (New York: Dutton, 2021), 178.
3. James Clear describes the process of creating friction in his book *Atomic Habits: An Easy & Proven Way to Build Good Habits & Break Bad Ones* (New York: Avery, 2018), 157.
4. In our book *Boundaries for Your Soul*, my coauthor and I described how numbing is related to "firefighting." Numbing occurs when a part of you rushes in to put out the flames of pain. See Alison Cook and Kimberly Miller, *Boundaries for Your Soul: How to Turn Your Overwhelming Thoughts and Feelings into Your Greatest Allies* (Nashville: Nelson Books, 2018), 34.
5. Melissa Dittmann, "Anger Across the Gender Divide," *Monitor on Psychology* 34, no. 3 (March 2003): 52, https://www.apa.org/monitor/mar03/angeracross.

6. Ecclesiastes 3:4.

7. Lembke, *Dopamine Nation*, 145.

Chapter 7: I Shouldn't Feel Ashamed of My Body

1. Early psychologists tended to disregard the role of the body in psychological processes and instead focused primarily on addressing behaviors, feelings, or thoughts. In more recent years, however, the field of psychology has increasingly expanded to acknowledge the significance of the body to our emotional and mental health. See J. C. Overholser, "50 Years of Psychotherapy: Erudition, Evolution, and Evaluation," *Journal of Contemporary Psychotherapy* 50 (2020): 87–93, https://doi.org/10.1007/s10879-019-09441-8.

2. For more on the mind-body connection, see Peter A. Levine, *In an Unspoken Voice: How the Body Releases Trauma and Restores Goodness* (Berkeley, CA: North Atlantic Books, 2010); Stephen Porges, *The Polyvagal Theory: Neurophysiological Foundations of Emotions, Attachment, Communication, and Self-Regulation* (New York: W. W. Norton, 2011); and Pat Ogden, *Trauma and the Body: A Sensorimotor Approach to Psychotherapy* (New York: W. W. Norton, 2006).

3. Ephesians 2:10.

4. 1 Corinthians 6:19.

5. Aundi Kolber, *Strong Like Water: Finding the Freedom, Safety, and Compassion to Move Through Hard Things—and Experience True Flourishing* (Carol Stream, IL: Tyndale House, 2023), 18.

6. For more on the nervous system and its role in healing from trauma, please check out the work of therapist Aundi Kolber: *Try Softer: A Fresh Approach to Move Us Out of Anxiety, Stress, and Survival Mode—and into a Life of Connection and Joy* (Carol Stream, IL: Tyndale House, 2020); and *Strong Like Water*.

7. Arlin Cuncic, "What Is 4–7–8 Breathing?," *Verywell Mind*, October 26, 2021, https://www.verywellmind.com/what-is-4-7-8-breathing-5204438.

8. You can find a free guided imagery audio exercise on my website at www.dralisoncook.com/ifsbundle/ or on any online meditation app such as InsightTimer or Ritual.io. To learn more about guided

imagery, see Jo Nash, "Guided Imagery in Therapy: 20 Powerful Scripts and Techniques," PositivePsychology.com, February 16, 2023, https://positivepsychology.com/guided-imagery-scripts/.

9. Tchiki Davis, "What Are Grounding Techniques?," *Psychology Today*, August 31, 2022, https://www.psychologytoday.com/us/blog/click -here-for-happiness/202208/what-are-grounding-techniques.

10. For more on the benefits of nature, see Michael Easter, *The Comfort Crisis: Embrace Discomfort to Reclaim Your Wild, Happy, Healthy Self* (New York: Rodale, 2021); and Rachel J. Hopman et al., "Resting-State Posterior Alpha Power Changes with Prolonged Exposure in a Natural Environment," *Cognitive Research: Principles and Implications* 5, no. 51 (October 27, 2020), https://doi.org/10.1186/s41235-020-00247-0.

11. Docetism and Gnosticism both taught that as matter, the body was bad or even evil, a position vehemently refuted by St. Augustine, among other early church fathers. "Docetism," *Britannica*, accessed October 11, 2023, https://www.britannica.com/topic/Docetism.

12. Genesis 1:27.

13. 1 Corinthians 6:19–20 MSG.

14. For more on the embodiment of Jesus, listen to episodes 45 and 46 of *The Best of You* podcast, a two-part conversation with Aundi Kolber.

15. Luke 24:13–32; John 20:19–23.

16. Luke 24:51; Acts 1:9–11.

17. 2 Samuel 6:14 NLT.

Chapter 8: I Shouldn't Feel Less Than Other People

1. Leon Festinger, "A Theory of Social Comparison Processes," *Human Relations* 7, no. 2 (1954): 117–40, https://doi.org/10.1177/0018726 75400700202.

2. Adele Samra, Wayne A. Warburton, and Andrew M. Collins, "Social Comparisons: A Potential Mechanism Linking Problematic Social Media Use with Depression," *Journal of Behavioral Addictions* 11, no. 2 (June 2022): 607–14, https://doi.org/10.1556/2006.2022.00023.

3. Katerina Lup, Leora Trub, and Lisa Rosenthal, "Instagram #Instasad?: Exploring Associations Among Instagram Use,

Depressive Symptoms, Negative Social Comparison, and Strangers Followed," *Cyberpsychology, Behavior, and Social Networking* 18, no. 5 (May 2015): 247–52, https://doi.org/10.1089/cyber.2014.0560.

4. Romans 2:4.

5. Kristin Neff, "The Physiology of Self-Compassion," Self-Compassion, accessed August 15, 2023, https://self-compassion.org/the-physiology -of-self-compassion.

6. For more on near and far enemies, see Dr. Chris Germer, "The Near and Far Enemies of Fierce Compassion," Mindfulness Teacher Training, October 22, 2020, mbsr.website/news/near-and-far-enemies -fierce-compassion.

7. Philippians 2:3.

8. Mark 12:31.

9. John 6:1–14.

10. You can learn more about CliftonStrengths assessments at https:// www.gallup.com/cliftonstrengths/en/252137/home.aspx.

11. Chen Yang and Rixin Tang, "Validating the 'Two Faces' of Envy: The Effect of Self-Control," *Frontiers in Psychology* 12 (October 27, 2021), https://doi.org/10.3389/fpsyg.2021.731451.

12. Amos 7:8.

Chapter 9: I Shouldn't Feel Trapped in Toxicity

1. Galatians 5:22–23 ESV.

2. Free 24-7 confidential sexual assault hotline: 1-800-656-HOPE, www.rainn.org; free 24-7, confidential domestic violence hotline: 1-800-799-SAFE, www.thehotline.org.

3. Tom Wright, *Matthew for Everyone, Part 1: Chapters 1–15*, 2nd ed. (Louisville, KY: Westminster John Knox Press, 2004), 51–52.

4. Matthew 10:16 ESV.

5. Song of Songs 8:6–7.

Chapter 10: I Shouldn't Feel Mad at My Loved One

1. For more on Dunbar's number, see Sheon Han, "You Can Only Maintain So Many Close Friendships," *The Atlantic*, May 20, 2021,

https://www.theatlantic.com/family/archive/2021/05/robin
-dunbar-explains-circles-friendship-dunbars-number/618931/.

2. Katie Shonk, "Interpersonal Conflict Resolution: Beyond Conflict
Avoidance," *Daily Blog* (blog), Harvard Law School, April 24, 2023,
www.pon.harvard.edu/daily/conflict-resolution/interpersonal
-conflict-resolution-beyond-conflict-avoidance/.

3. Logan Ury, "Want to Improve Your Relationships? Start Paying
More Attention to Bids," The Gottman Institute, accessed
September 26, 2023, https://www.gottman.com/blog/want-to
-improve-your-relationship-start-paying-more-attention-to-bids/.

Chapter 11: I Shouldn't Feel Conflicted About God

1. Elizabeth Bernstein, "The Science of Prayer," *Wall Street Journal*,
May 17, 2020, https://www.wsj.com/articles/the-science-of-prayer
-11589720400.

2. Matthew 7:9–11.

3. I first heard this term from Dr. Curt Thompson through various
personal conversations and his writings.

4. Romans 5:3–5.

5. Galatians 5:22–23 ESV.

6. Mark 9:24.

7. Mark 14:36.

8. Job 13:15.

9. Psalm 42:5.

10. I first learned this phrase from the book by Stanley Hauerwas,
*With the Grain of the Universe: The Church's Witness and Natural
Theology* (Grand Rapids: Baker Academic, 2013).

11. For a beautiful resource on holistic spiritual practices, see Kayla
Craig, *Every Season Sacred: Reflections, Prayers, and Invitations to
Nourish Your Soul and Nurture Your Family Throughout the Year*
(Carol Stream, IL: Tyndale House, 2023).

12. Philippians 2:12.

13. Curt Thompson, *The Soul of Desire: Discovering the Neuroscience of*

Longing, Beauty, and Community (Downers Grove, IL: InterVarsity, 2021), 98.

14. Thompson, *Soul of Desire*, 96.

Conclusion: The Paradox of Hope

1. Deb Dana coined the term "glimmer." For more on glimmers, see *The Polyvagal Theory in Therapy: Engaging the Rhythm of Regulation* (New York: W. W. Norton, 2018).
2. Romans 5:3–5.
3. For a beautiful exposition of the neurobiology of hope, see Curt Thompson, *The Deepest Place: Suffering and the Formation of Hope* (Grand Rapids: Zondervan, 2023).

About the Author

Dr. Alison Cook is a therapist and host of the top-ranked *The Best of You* podcast. She is the author of the ECPA bestselling book *The Best of You* and coauthor of *Boundaries for Your Soul*. Widely recognized as an expert at the intersection of faith and psychology, Dr. Alison empowers individuals to heal from past wounds, develop a strong sense of self, forge healthy relationships, and experience a loving God who is for them. She and her husband, Joe, are the parents of two adult children. They call both Boston and Wyoming home. Connect with Dr. Alison at www.dralisoncook.com.